HOW TO FIX SUPER

BAD EGG

ANDREW BRAGG

connorcourt
PUBLISHING

CONNOR COURT PUBLISHING PTY LTD
PO Box 7257
Redland Bay QLD 4165
sales@connorcourt.com
www.connorcourt.com

Front cover design: Ian James

ISBN: 978-1-925826-89-0 (pbk.)

Printed in Australia

Dedicated to the workers of Australia

CONTENTS

FOREWORD

It's always good to invest in policy ideas. Super is one of the biggest ideas in Australia.

Few understand superannuation well and the industry has revelled in its opacity for 30 years.

It is Australia's biggest closed shop.

The point of this short book is not to have an ideological discussion. It is to encourage the nation to change direction on super. Not to junk it, but to make it work.

Put simply, if it isn't working, why are we doing it?

As Australia faces the Coronavirus (COVID-19), it is clear the nation cannot afford indulgences that do not work.

Superannuation will be put in the spotlight like never before.

Australians will rightly ask, can I access my super if I am sick? Workers and small businesses will ask why am I paying super when I desperately need money now?

The industry's answer will always be that super funds should have more super money to manage. They are the most conflicted organisations in Australia.

The super system costs more than it saves. Surely, that is not the idea of super.

This short book contains some of the answers to these questions.

One positive factor arising from COVID-19 is the nation will now have a hard discussion on super. This should have happened 30 years ago.

INTRODUCTION

Superannuation is a great idea: a policy to reduce the cost of an aging population and boost the quality of life of Australians in retirement. It is also a huge and radical experiment: a significant intervention against free and private choice, based on the idea that government knows best.

In other words, an idea with good intentions which contains enormous trade-offs for Australians and Australia.

Superannuation, as an idea, has not been supported with a clear objective and framework for achieving the purpose. It is failing workers, it is failing Australian taxpayers.

A great idea will remain just an idea if it isn't supported by the machinery necessary to deliver on the purpose.

By creating a hugely complex retirement income system, a good idea becomes a burden on the economy. The three key pillars of the system – government funded age pension, compulsory superannuation and voluntary savings interacting constantly with each other which is often confusing.[1]

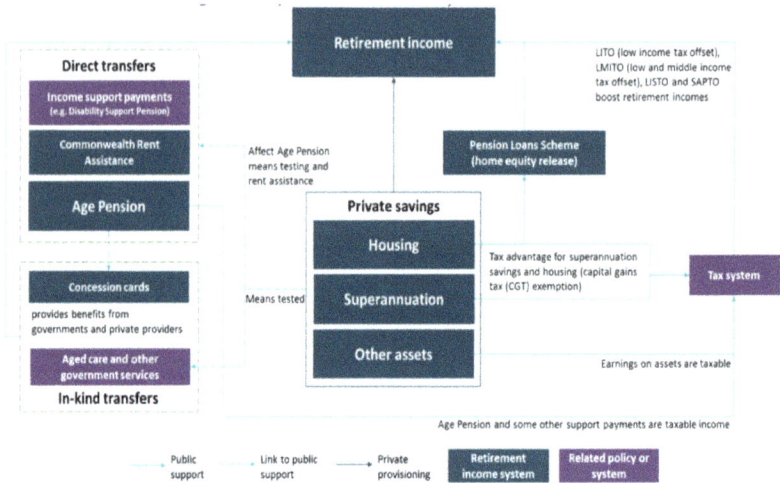

Source: Treasury

The purpose of this monograph is to set out a clear purpose for superannuation, assess the current scheme and consider better options for the future.

I undertake this task as a partisan, as a Senator for New South Wales and a member of the Morrison Government and the Liberal Party of Australia.

These are my own views about the scheme's direction and should not be confused with the opinion of anyone else, nor as an official policy of the Liberal Party.

If this monograph moves the debate toward how super can be improved, I would regard it as a success.

The main points are:

1. For 30 years, the debate on superannuation has been tainted by the self-interest of financial institutions, privileged unions and employer groups;

2. Super was conceived by the trade unions, for the union movement and delivered by their political arm, the Labor Party. The system is on track to pay $31m per annum to the unions by 2030;

3. Addressing the myth making of the superannuation industry and its related party vested interests is a modern Modest Member cause;

4. There exists a "Great Super Gap" and there should be more honesty about what super can and cannot achieve;

5. A clear objective for super should be established, because it costs more than it saves;

6. Superannuation has always been an enormous trade off for workers – it always will be;

7. Super must work harder for Australians - a target for 50 per cent of Australians to become self-funded retirees should be adopted;

8. The market structure requires drastic surgery, including considering the use of the Future Fund;

9. More flexibility is needed to the system to deliver for Australians who are not homogenous; and

10. The system ought to be fixed rather than discarded at this juncture.

1

BIG MONEY

What are we trying to achieve with this extraordinary experiment of superannuation?

Few people know what the core objective is. Yet we compel people to save almost 10 per cent of their salaries and wages.

The truth is the idea of self-funded or largely self-funded retirement has been a shared vision for the two parties, albeit with different ideas of delivery.

Centre right governments sought to introduce national insurance in the 1920s and 1930s but failed. As Dallas McInerney told the Sydney Institute in 2011:

> A report led to Treasurer Page introducing the National Insurance Bill in 1928, but the legislation failed to gain parliamentary approval before the defeat of the government later that year. In fact, the issue was to prove problematic for the non- Labor side of Australian politics, with Menzies citing Prime Minister Joe Lyon's prevarication on the National Insurance Scheme as the (ostensible) reason for his resignation from the government in 1939.

Menzies, perhaps more than any other Australian leader, thought deeply about who he represented as he formulated the Liberal Party of Australia throughout the 1940s.

A cornerstone of the Menzies approach was support for the underrepresented and poorly organised middle classes. This manifested into policies to drive home ownership to historical highs but also into ideas to drive middle class security – through ideas like national insurance.

With national insurance defeated in 1961, the formalisation of a scheme beyond the age pension stalled for another two decades with the notable exception of an investigation into national insurance by Whitlam in his madcap years.

Whitlam's Labor Minister Jim McClelland asked former Labor advisor and Supreme Court judge, Howard Nathan, to help investigate setting up a national savings scheme as well as commissioning the Hancock review into National Superannuation. After testing the waters in Western Australia, South Australia and Victoria, Nathan reported there was no support and that "they thought I was on a mission from Lenin. I reported this and was assailed yet again."

This radical idea went into the sand for another decade.

Eventually Bob Hawke's accord with the trade unions in the mid-1980s provided an informal mechanism for kicking super off in a formal sense. Paul Keating's government legislated super in 1992 with the onus on employers to make the compulsory contribution.

Today's superannuation scheme maintains its Labor-sponsored birth certificate. Mary Easson freely admits in her book on the history of super that "the modern Australian superannuation system was developed from the creative foresight of its founders, principally those in the unions and the Labor Government."[1]

Former Labor Treasurer Chris Bowen has described super as a "long term Labor agenda."[2] Designed as a tax under the corporations constitutional head of power, the Superannuation Guarantee charge required a growing percentage of workers' salaries and wages to be paid to a complying fund. It started at 3 per cent after being passed by the Commonwealth Parliament in mid-1992.

The radical idea was finally airborne through a system of creeping contributions. Perhaps this made it seem less radical than it had appeared when earlier generations had rejected it.

Management of the scheme was given to the unions and the financial institutions despite a recommendation from the 1976 Hancock Review into National Superannuation to establish a government default fund.

As modern superannuation is a union project, it is unsurprising that the unions were given the keys to the scheme. This is a byproduct of the relationship between Paul Keating and his contemporary, the union boss Bill Kelty.

Kelty tells Easson a fellow ACTU staffer deserves much of the credit: "now Iain Ross did all the hard work. Ross, from the time he came into the ACTU was the intellectual catalyst and he was working with us."

Ross would maintain his connection to superannuation and industrial relations through his later appointment as President of the Fair Work Commission.

This radical economic policy, perhaps the largest Australian economic experiment, was born without any clear objectives.

This is hardly surprising given the bizarre legal conception of super. Long serving Treasury official Paul Tilley wrote in his history of the Treasury Department that the super policy was wholly conceived by the backbench member Paul Keating.

Tilley says of the early 1990s, "Treasury was actually not well equipped to do the necessary long term modelling work." Further, he noted the head of the area responsible for the introduction of super Ian Robinson had drawn up the modelling on the "back of an envelope which had been thrown out!"[3]

Robinson told Tilley "Treasury was exposed as introducing a policy agenda with significant long term impacts that hadn't been modelled."[4]

Given the messy commencement, it is amazing that the system started under an Act of Federal Parliament in 1992: the Superannuation Guarantee Act.

As Prime Minister, Paul Keating introduced a scheme which

1. Provided broad coverage of the workforce
2. An avenue for Australians to become self-funded retirees
3. Ended the unaffordable, unsustainable defined benefit schemes

Like so many similar nations, Australia faces an aging population. We confront this aging population with a smaller taxpaying base relative to retirees. The economists call this the dependency ratio and it means the government's capacity to pay for things are threatened as the tax base shrinks.

It was set up as a "defined contribution" scheme, a system in which what goes in determines what comes out at the end plus earnings, less fees and tax.

Many comparable nations are still playing catch up as they face crippling costs of unfunded defined benefit schemes and the same unfavourable demographic profile.

The American public pension is illustrative of the pitfalls of defined benefit schemes. In America, most public-sector employees have a defined benefit scheme in the form of a pension linked to their final salary. Yet states are struggling to pay for such schemes. In 2014, pension costs accounted for 15 per cent of the budget in three states.[5]

Such high pension burdens have meant that states are contributing less than actuaries have said is necessary.

In 2009, the actuaries for the Illinois Teachers scheme recommended $2.1 billion in contributions; the state paid $1.6 billion. In 2018, the actuaries recommended $7.1 billion but the state paid only $4.2 billion.[6]

Australia must avoid being in such a precarious situation at all costs. But we should never confuse big with successful. Having a $3 trillion system does not necessarily indicate success – especially when we are operating without a clear objective.

Super: A Bug Business

Why does super matter? Because super is on its way to dominate the economy. The total value of assets in Australia's superannuation system is $2.8 trillion, which is about 150 per cent of GDP.

The current pool of superannuation funds under management is roughly 1.4 times the size of Australian equities market capitalisation as at June 2019.

Superannuation funds under management are expected to reach $5.0 trillion by 2029, or 160 per cent of GDP in that year, ultimately rising to 180 per cent of GDP 20 years later.

Actuarial Firm Rice Warner also expects Australian super funds will own 20 per cent of all listed Australian companies by 2034. This places a huge burden on a sector which has often struggled to act maturely.

A hive of vested interests

Few Australian schemes have given life to the famous quip of Former New South Wales Premier Jack Lang: "in the great race of life, always back self-interest, at least you know it's trying."

The super industry works terribly hard for vested interests – principally financial institutions and unions. For a system of such fundamental importance to Australia's economy and society, it often acts contrary to the interest of one noticeable group – Australians.

This is evident in the structures of the funds and the way ancient laws and customs have been religiously maintained since superannuation started under Commonwealth law in 1992.

Australia's only compulsory product has behaved as any privileged industry would. There are lurks and layers and layers of intermediation.

The superannuation funds do not perform many tasks. They are effectively shell companies. Almost every task is outsourced to fund managers, administrators, custodians, asset consultants and insurers. There are very few super funds that do anything internally.

There are two main types of pooled funds: industry and retail.

The retail funds have generally underperformed and are riven with conflicts. The Hayne Royal Commission destroyed the credibility of the retail funds after it was demonstrated many large funds regularly put the members last. Equally, the COVID-19 crisis has destroyed the credibility of several industry funds after their industry representatives sought a government bailout amid fears of illiquidity.

Industry funds

Anyone who has looked into the industry super system will appreciate the intricate alliance between industry super funds, the union movement and the Labor Party.

The super funds provide the money, the union movement provide the people and the Labor Party provides the parliamentary representation.

The super system has done exactly what venerated Hawke era Finance Minister Peter Walsh feared. He said "consistent with its policy of putting the interests of those with jobs ahead of those without jobs, the ACTU was in favor of compulsory superannuation... (for lower income workers) it will be a cost ineffective investment ... but are a pot of gold for those, including unions, who can get into super fund management."[7]

This team really has some chemistry. Payments from industry super funds to unions have increased dramatically over the past 10 years whilst union membership has fallen.

In 2006-2007, industry super paid unions $3.22 million, in 2011 it was $7.02 million and in 2017, it was a whopping $10.45 million. A normalised growth rate of 9 per cent year on year was paid out of industry funds to unions.

A straight line forecast based on over 10 years of historical data predicts over $31.4 million will be paid to unions by industry funds by 2030. This represents a greater than 200 per cent increase on today's transfers to unions. Note that unions are not poor – they have more than $1.5 billion in assets.[8]

FIGURE 2: INDUSTRY SUPER PAYMENTS TO UNIONS

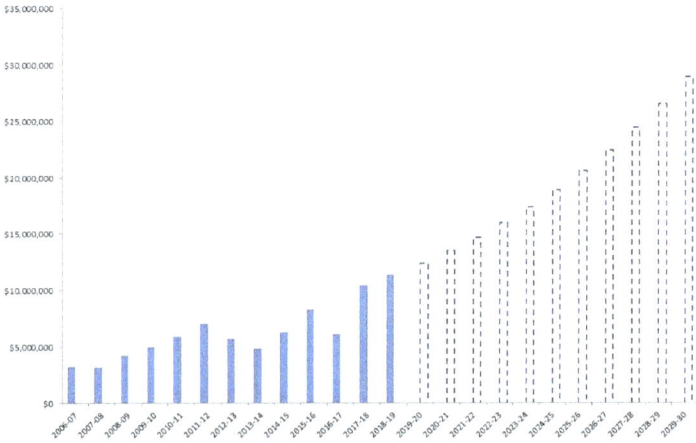

Source: Australian Electoral Commission

TABLE 1: INDUSTRY SUPER PAYMENTS TO UNIONS

Year	Amount
2006-07	$3,220,174
2007-08	$3,167,200
2008-09	$4,250,247
2009-10	$4,972,405
2010-11	$5,913,790
2011-12	$7,016,691
2012-13	$5,729,650
2013-14	$4,855,893
2014-15	$6,302,450
2015-16	$8,314,787
2016-17	$6,092,212
2017-18	$10,446,168
2018-19	$11,370,862
2019-20	*$12,377,410*
2020-21	*$13,473,057*
2021-22	*$14,665,691*
2022-23	*$15,963,896*
2023-24	*$17,377,019*
2024-25	*$18,915,231*
2025-26	*$20,589,606*
2026-27	*$22,412,196*
2027-28	*$24,396,122*
2028-29	*$26,555,664*
2029-30	*$28,906,369*
2030-31	*$31,465,159*

Source: Australian Electoral Commission

$80 million of retirement savings has been paid directly to unions; it is ballooning.

The $31 million projection of annual payments from industry funds to unions is a conservative estimate. It is based on the AEC data which does not capture all the payments. It solely captures payments made to unions which are affiliated with the Australian Labor Party and therefore classified as "registered organisations".

Make no mistake, industry super funds are on track to be the biggest political donors in Australia. They'll be bigger than the CFMMEU and Co.

It does not include other forms of largesse which the trustees of the funds spend on themselves such as a $20 million entertainment and marketing expense incurred by industry fund HostPlus exposed in the Hayne Royal Commission.

Unions play an important role in Australian life, especially in the protection of lower income workers. However in recent years, too many unions have shown they cannot be trusted with workers' money.

During the Heydon Royal Commission, issues relating to one major super fund in relation to data protection and the privacy of employers contributing to that fund arose. In giving evidence to the Royal Commission, some of the officials from that fund were found to have given evidence which conflicted other evidence which the Royal Commission had gathered. This led to certain prosecutions.

For example, Kathy Jackson, former National Secretary of the Health Services Union, was ordered to pay $1.4 million in compensation to the union for misappropriating funds. According to the union, they alleged she funnelled the money into an opulent lifestyle, including luxury goods, artwork, fine wine and dining on holidays, artwork and other luxuries. As of June 2015 Jackson was facing 164 criminal theft and fraud charges.

Union officials using union money for their personal gain is not new. The Transport Workers' Union officials bought $150,000 American utes for their use. Their buddies at the National Union of Workers spent $650,000 on tattoos, Botox, cruises, divorce lawyers and weight loss surgery.[9]

Unions are some of the largest political donors in Australia. The Electrical Trades Union was the single largest political donor in the country in the 2019 election cycle.[10]

The disproportionate influence unions have on Australian public life occurs because of their substantial financial resources. Sadly, unions are all too often arguing for economic policies which would undermine workers' interests.

In the past decade unions have argued against trade deals, tax cuts and policies to promote investment in Australia.

Workers' superannuation should not be providing the financial resources for unions to advocate anti-worker policies.

Retail funds

The retail funds have shown they are very focused on themselves – shareholders and management, at the expense of workers.

Retail funds racked up billions in fines and customer remediation after Hayne Banking Royal Commission.

Hayne showed there are significant conflicts of interest.

This stems from the vertical integration of the wealth management industry, where many banks have one subsidiary providing financial advice and another selling financial products.

The 'one stop shop' provides customers with added convenience as they only have to deal with one financial institution. Yet this model also presents serious issues. The Productivity Commission Report commenting that:

> The 'one stop shop' model creates a bias towards promoting the owner's products above others, even where they may not be ideal for the consumer.[11]

Historically, this conflict has been rampant in the Australian retail superannuation sector. Some of the largest retail superannuation funds have been owned and operated by the big four banks. These include BT, Colonial First State and MLC which were owned by Westpac, CBA and NAB respectively.

The large client base and broad range of financial products at the disposal of banks has proven to be a conflicted combination. Retail super funds can leverage their banking relationships to target vulnerable, unsophisticated clients.

A major ASIC investigation found that 68 per cent of retail superannuation customers invest in in-house products after receiving advice from an advisor employed at a retail super fund. Yet only 21 per cent of a retail super fund's product list are in-house products.[12]

The stories are telling.

Colonial First State provided members with interest rates lower than even the official Reserve Bank cash rate for its cash-only investment options.

Kenneth Hayne's Royal Commission exposed a "fees for no service" scandal where superannuation members were charged for no service rendered. Some estimates had these figures as high as $1 billion.

Walkley winning journalist Adele Ferguson said of the hearings:

> Over twenty days of grueling hearings, the royal commission had demonstrated how trustees in superannuation retail funds had sat in conflicted silence around boardroom tables, earning tidy sums as they rubber stamped a myriad of schemes designed to squeeze as many fees out of members as possible.

MLC charged a 'plan service fee' of up to 1.5 per cent for the opportunity to access a financial adviser, irrespective of whether the advice was actually provided. The corporate regulator ASIC alleges MLC charged $100 million in fees where no advice service was provided.

An AMP executive even admitted during the Royal Commission that "It's clear that we preference the interests of shareholders… at the expense of clients."[13]

Super has been a gravy train for industry and retail funds to make a motza for unions or financial institutions.

The immediate future looks much brighter.

Financial services regulation is a key policy focus of the Morrison Government. Treasurer Josh Frydenberg has led the way, stating that:

The government is taking action on all 76 recommendations contained in the final report of the royal commission and will continue to take the necessary steps to restore trust in Australia's financial system.[114]

No other comparable reform process has been implemented in a timetable this tight.

The report was presented to the government on 1 February 2019. The Treasurer responded within 3 days.

Of the 76 recommendations, 54 are directed at the government - with 40 requiring legislation.

The Treasurer says that by the middle of 2021, 90 per cent of the commitments will be implemented or before Parliament.

This means we will have delivered the Hayne reform plan in two and a half years – a significant restructuring of one of Australia's largest industries.

One of the first pieces of legislation that has already passed Parliament is the abolition of adviser commissions. This sailed through the Parliament in late 2019.

This means that financial advisers will no longer be remunerated through never ending trail commissions which distort advice given to retail clients. Advisers will only be remunerated through a fee for service model under our reforms.

Another reform is the end of inducements for super trustees.

As emerged during the Royal Commission, many super fund executives were being wined and dined to secure business.

The so called "HostPlus" clause was swiftly legislated by the Morrison government after the *Australian Financial Review* reported:

> Commissioner Kenneth Hayne recommended changing super laws to prohibit the 'treating of employers'. He cited the $21.44 million that Hostplus spent on marketing including corporate hospitality, in 2017. This included entertaining chief executives of Hostplus employers at the Australian Open.

This sort of largesse is now over thanks to our new laws. Overall, the "rorts" and rip offs painfully illustrate how super funds do not put their members interests first.

These incidents are not flashes in the pan. There is an ingrained culture of privilege which cannot be resolved with a bill or two.

2

CONFLICTS

One of the biggest flaws in this policy area is the lack of independent analysis.

Although the superannuation industry was created under government mandate, it has consistently relied on the support of wealthy advocacy groups to advance its interests. I know because I worked inside this industry for seven years.

In contrast when the Superannuation Guarantee (SG) debate unfolded in the Senate during the period of 1991-94, consumer advocacy groups played a major role in how the system should be built.

Eva Cox of the Womens' Economic Think Tank said during the 1992 debate:

> . . . this is a deal between the Government and the ACTU about something which has got very little to do with retirement income and much more to do with the politics of the union movement and the Government.

The Australian Council of Social Services (ACOSS) for example advocated that SG was unsuited to low income workers as they need the money when it is earned, not later. In 2020, ACOSS again voiced their concern that the SG system was a blunt instrument and may not be suited to lower income Australians by saying:

> ... an increase in the SG is a bad deal for people with low incomes, assuming most of the SG comes from low pay rises.
>
> They are forced to save to reach a living standard post-retirement that's often higher than the one they had through working life, part of the benefit is (appropriately) clawed back via the age pension income test, and they get little or no tax support for their saving efforts.

These interventions have been rare.

Over the three decades of the SG system, the consumer group Choice has been active on fees, charges and commissions, and dispute resolution, advocating for better regulation. Regrettably, the advocacy is now mostly a series of salvoes between the retail and the industry funds, who have the resources to 'muscle out' other interested viewpoints. I deal with the culture war later.

Reports, articles and media appearances from vested interest groups which support the superannuation system makes it difficult to critically assess whether the system is working.

As the world becomes increasingly data-driven, the old myths will be harder to maintain. This is a good development as it's getting harder to hide behind spin.

A casual observer may think super is going to both pay for

everyone's retirement in full and obviate the need for an age pension.

Sadly, these myths are simply not true.

There are four large advocacy groups which claim to represent superannuation funds or perhaps their members. Each group has at least 15 staff and a considerable budget for research and marketing.

The principal activities include commissioning modelling, being constantly decamped at Parliament House in Canberra, writing opinion pieces for the various newspapers and running adverts on different media outlets.

One of the groups spends more than $20 million a year on advertising.[1] One particular industry body spent $3.5 million of retirement savings in the first quarter of 2020 to argue for higher contributions (into their coffers).[2]

Sometimes, despite the scale of the resources being put into advocacy, odd results are generated.

At a Senate Economics Committee public hearing I chaired in 2019, the industry's advocates were embarrassingly exposed.

The hearings were conducted to consider a relatively straightforward once off amnesty for employers struggling to meet their complicated superannuation obligations.

The result, two of the bodies said they supported it and two said they did not!

This is despite the significant overlap in the membership of the bodies, making it unclear to say the least how there could be different views presented.

No one should be surprised that superannuation associations will argue for their industry. That is not a problem. The problem the nation faces on superannuation is that too few of the voices in the debate have clean hands.

The scale of both the individual and the nation's investment in super demands an honest debate.

Yet a $3 trillion system has long tentacles. The layers and layers of intermediation from the trustees through to custodians, asset managers, administrators and insurers have often been deployed to shut down debates and critics.

I have first-hand experience. Before I was elected to the Commonwealth Parliament, I was working for the Business Council of Australia (BCA).

Throughout its history, the BCA has not generally supported compulsory superannuation.

I had been writing articles in the *Daily Telegraph* throughout 2017 which outlined the super funds were making considerable payments to trade unions without disclosure to consumers.

The lobby group, Industry Super Australia, wrote letters to each of the chief executives of the BCA to try and secure my silence.

The articles suggested these payments ought to be disclosed in the interests of transparency as they would hit $22 million a year by 2025 and it was in the public interest.

Childish letter writing is a standard bullyboy tactic. Attempting to put a critic's job at risk is just shameful.

Thankfully the BCA's leadership of Jennifer Westacott and Grant King stood by me.

The net result of this activity is there are few, certainly within the finance sector that are willing to have a proper debate about how the system is travelling.

The other result is that many Parliamentarians "run the lines" from the industry without thinking.

This has been a real problem for the Parliamentary Labor Party which has not invested in independent policy formulation in recent years. Almost every policy proposal is designed to increase the flow of funds into industry super funds at the expense of other fund structures or investments such as houses.

This dangerous approach exploded in Labor's face during the 2019 election with Labor's policy to abolish refundable franking credits, otherwise known as the Retiree Tax. This unfair and retrospective policy damaged Labor during the election according to Labor's official campaign review.

I have no doubt that the policy was originally proposed by the industry super funds as a way to increase market share and was later adopted by the Labor Party.

The tax would have severely damaged self-managed super funds (SMSFs) as they would have lost access to the cash refunds they deserve for effectively being double taxed. This is because self-managed funds must segregate their assets between the accumulation and pension phase.

Contrastingly, large funds, like industry funds, are structured in a way which allows the tax position of accumulation members to support retired members.

Large funds do not like SMSFs because they take large balances from industry and retail funds as they offer more flexibility and control.

Finding ways to throw regulation in the path of SMSFs is not therefore new! The industry super movement fell over themselves to back in Labor's policy.

They even stuck with it through its multiple iterations which were required.

For example, AustralianSuper switched its position on franking credits in the space of a few years, to back in Labor's policy as *The Australian* revealed during the last election. In 2015, AustralianSuper said:

> AustralianSuper submits that there are substantial benefits to Australia in the continued operation of the present dividend imputation system. AustralianSuper strongly supports the dividend imputation system and opposes modification or removal of the system.

Yet during the 2019 election campaign they said:

> Having carefully considered the publicly available material about this proposed change [abolishment of refundable franking credits], we are satisfied it won't lead to significant adverse capital flows or negative impacts on members' long-term balances.[3]

In other words, the change won't affect AustralianSuper. But it will affect the 1 million Australians who have SMSFs.[4]

Labor adopted someone else's policy which was designed to build market share for a particular sector. That was silly.

It serves as a warning to Parliamentarians: be careful. Don't get trapped in the super industry's advocacy leviathan.

The leviathan will only grow. There are so many Parliamentarians with close links to the industry super funds and their union owners. This remains a great danger for Labor as I observe their Senators and Members of Parliament "run the lines" of the industry super funds on a daily basis.

Labor MPs run industry super's lines on imputation changes, the super amnesty, COVID-19 access measures and dozens of minor regulatory changes. They are inseparable.

During the 2019 election, Industry Super Australia worked quietly behind the scenes to support their Labor allies, stating that Labor's proposed dividend imputation changes 'will have little or no impact on the super of most Australians.'[5] Thankfully, the new tax was defeated at the ballot box.[6]

The only antidote is independent thought and independent policy formulation.

For the first 28 years of compulsory super, the main participants in the debate on super were the funds themselves, insurers, asset managers, unions and the industry bodies.

In recent years, there has been a growth of non-conflicted parties that have taken an interest in super as it has swelled to eclipse the economy, the nation's budget and the capitalisation of the securities exchange.

I welcome the entry of groups such as the Grattan Institute, the Centre for Independent Studies and academics who have undertaken detailed and serious research which hasn't been commissioned by the industry.

As the 2020s kick off, outsiders are starting to take notice. Much of the analysis is unflattering. Sydney University academic Dr Cameron Murray estimates compulsory super has eaten the equivalent of 2 per cent of GDP – around $40 billion per annum – from the economy.

Dr Murray says: "Scrapping the super system would massively improve Australia's economic performance – it's costly and inefficient, unnecessary, and incredibly unfair," he said.

> Instead of channelling incomes through asset markets, decreasing demand and soaking up a workforce the size of the military on an accounting exercise, the 28 million superannuation account holders could spend up to an additional $20,000 per year.[7]

Independent researchers in the private sector and the Treasury have an important role in presenting the information policymakers need to make balanced decisions free of the industry's myths and long arms.

A Modern Modest Member Issue

In so many ways, the myth making of the superannuation industry is similar to the myths propagated in an earlier age about industry protection.

The two similarities are: one, a slew of Parliamentarians totally besotted with the status quo and two, the heavying elements of industry.

On the former, the Modest Member himself, Bert Kelly, said in 1986:

> I became the Member for Wakefield in 1958. My tariff campaign started the next year in 1959. At the beginning I fought for lower trade barriers because I knew that the cost of tariff protection was bone, in the end, by exporters. And as mine was a farming electorate, it was natural for me to try and get tariffs lowered. The only thing that puzzled me was why other members with rural electorates did not seem to worry about it like I did.

Kelly said of the industry efforts in 1979:

> The other reason why we do not reduce tariffs as we should is that governments are clay in the hands of the pressure groups.
>
> GMH can scare out governments by threatening to dismiss people if the government does not give its milk down and continue to subsidise the industry at a ruinous cost to the community, and incidentally make the cars too dear to buy...
>
> Australian politicians are always terrified of pressure groups, particularly those with loud voices.[8]

Kelly forged ahead with his tariff campaign, often in a lonely manner. But ultimately more people inside and outside Parliament understood the damaging cost of industry protection.

Government reports such as the Vernon Committee of 1965 were critical in establishing a base to move forward with better policies.

This is the role that Treasury inquires such as the Retirement Income Review should fulfil alongside periodic studies like the Intergenerational Report series.

More than any other report, the Intergenerational Report (IGR) should be used as a basis to heavily scrutinise our investment in super.

The parallel between tariffs and super is imperfect because Kelly was on a mission to achieve a particular outcome: the abolition of protectionism.

In the contemporary case of super, the mission is far less brutal: the recalibration of superannuation so that it works harder for workers.

3

OBJECTIVES

Unfortunately, super was proposed as a solution to many problems at the outset. This has dogged the scheme for 30 years. The system costs more than it saves the budget. It may never deliver a positive affect on the Budget.

TABLE 2: THE NET COST OF THE SUPERANNUATION GUARANTEE

The net cost of the superannuation guarantee system is around 0.47 per cent of GDP in 2019. It remains net negative to budget until 2060 and possibly beyond.

% OF GDP	NET ANNUAL FISCAL EFFECT	EXPENSE SAVE	TAX LOSS
2019	-0.471	0.213	-0.683
2020	-0.471	0.218	-0.688
2021	-0.447	0.228	-0.673
2022	-0.452	0.233	-0.688
2023	-0.452	0.232	-0.683
2024	-0.427	0.242	-0.669
2025	-0.437	0.252	-0.683
2026	-0.437	0.262	-0.698
2027	-0.413	0.272	-0.688
2028	-0.403	0.281	-0.688
2029	-0.378	0.291	-0.669
2030	-0.378	0.301	-0.679

Source: Grattan Institute

The purported objectives have included to deliver:

1. Better retirement standards
2. Reduced age pension costs
3. Higher national savings
4. Reduced reliance on foreign capital

These are the four primary justifications outlined by proponents of the system. It is regularly argued that all four factors would be more favourable were the Superannuation Guarantee contribution increased to 12 per cent or beyond.

Retirement standards

A better standard of life in retirement is the starting point. The benchmark used is the age pension. The age pension provides an income of around $24,000 for a person. This is about 27 per cent of average weekly earnings.

Currently, 68 per cent of retirees still take some form of pension – either part or full.[2] This finding from Treasury's Retirement Income Review is the first time the figure has budged from around 70 per cent reliance, which featured in the 2015 Intergenerational Report.

The super and social security systems are calibrated so that the more super a retiree has, the lower their pension will be until a retiree hits a ceiling where no part pension is payable based on an assets test.

The promise of a higher retirement standard than the age pension can be tested by considering how much better the retirement years would be with super.

The superannuation industry says a modest lifestyle at age 65 is $27,000 and comfortable is $43,000. At the age of 85, the numbers fall to $26,000 and $41,000. If a retiree rightly desires a comfortable life in retirement, their super should ideally exceed the $41,000 benchmark.

Several factors complicate this assessment:

1. Retirement is a vastly flexible concept in 2019, compared to 1992. Retirees can access all forms of flexible work and the super scheme promotes flexibility and contributions much later into "retirement"

2. Age pensions reduce with higher super balances

A balance of $902,000 is required to achieve the industry comfortable target for a male who retires at 65 years and lives to 87. This is the figure required without the age pension. The figure would be significantly lower factoring in the age pension.

With average balances around $196,400 for men and $129,100 for women, super will only last for a few years of retirement.[2]

Research conducted for this book shows that 56 per cent of Australians do not believe they will be self-funded in retirement.

The fact remains, the intermingling of super with the pension system means this assessment is fraught. Accordingly, it cannot be claimed that super has heavily contributed to a higher standard of living for the masses. If it has, it's only for a few years.

As ACOSS says, the intermingling between the super scheme and age pension means a higher super balance may mean a lower pension payment which is a one step forward, two steps back move.

Reduced pension outlays
One of Keating's objectives has almost been achieved. Pension reliance is reducing. Around 68 per cent of Australians will take a pension today and keep doing so until 2055 according to the Treasury.[3]

There has been a downward trend in the share of those aged 65 and over receiving income support since the mid-1990s. This is as a result of policy changes, economic conditions and growing superannuation assets.

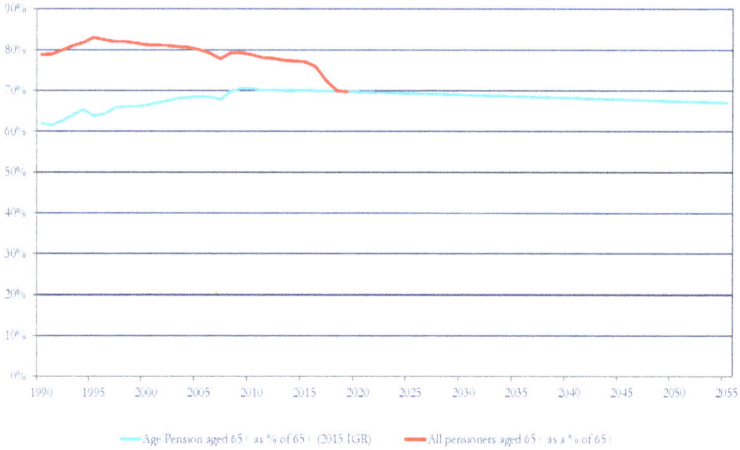

Source: Parliamentary Library

This is too low and we should be aiming for at least 50 per cent of Australians to become self-funded if the system is to be justified.

Leading actuary Michael Rice reports "the pension was about 2.9 per cent of GDP in 2002. It is now about 2.6 per cent of GDP and it could fall to close to 2 per cent by the end of the century."

Lower pension reliance has been aided by fewer people being eligible for a part pension in recent years, rather than superannuation driving the outcome.

Higher national savings

Paul Keating predicted in 1996 that the superannuation system would boost national savings from $230 billion to $2 trillion by 2020.[4]

Yet the truth is that superannuation has not boosted national savings. In the 1980s, Australia's gross domestic savings as a percentage of GDP consistently hovered around 26 per cent.

In 2018, this figure was 24.7 per cent.[5] This shows that the system has merely maintained a static level of savings as people have saved less as super swells. This is exactly what former Senator Richard Alston said during the 1992 debate in the Senate on the Superannuation Guarantee bill: "it cannot be said with any degree of confidence that there will be any particular level of increase in savings as a result of this regime."

During the pivotal 1992 Senate debate, Alston went on to predict a decline in national savings through a deliberate distortion of capital in Australia into the arms of the Keating Government's political allies:

> Indeed, it is possible that the Government's initiatives are exacerbating a major shift in savings away from traditional retail financial institutions. This structural shift of savings will have profound and largely unforeseen consequences for the composition of investment flows. Compulsory superannuation would hasten the process by allowing major taxation concessions for compulsory superannuation. National savings may actually decline.

The transaction costs in boosting private savings via increased levels of super savings are greater than the costs of more prudent budget savings by State and Commonwealth Governments.

The drive to reduce budget deficits and to strive for surpluses has in all likelihood played a more critical role in maintaining national savings.

Lower reliance on foreign capital

The same can be said on the claim made by the super industry that "Superannuation reduces reliance on foreign capital".[6]

Australia is still heavily reliant upon foreign investments, just as we were in 1992. Indeed, Australia's net inflow of foreign direct investment as a percentage of GDP has increased from almost 28 per cent to more than 55 per cent in 2019.[7]

Super is not reducing reliance on foreign capital but it is playing a role to reduce Australia's current account deficit.

In any event, there is nothing wrong with foreign investment, it has always been an important feature of our economy and society.

Recent current account surpluses have been achieved – the first since the 1970s. This has been used by the superannuation industry to argue the point that super is reducing our reliance on foreign capital, thereby extinguishing fears of a Banana Republic.

Reserve Bank of Australia Deputy Governor Guy Debelle outlined the main driver of the current account surplus is the favourable trade balance. He said of superannuation:

> For most of its modern history, foreigners owned more equity in Australian companies than Australians owned in foreign companies. But since 2013, that has not been true. Since 2013, Australians have owned more foreign equity than foreigners have owned Australian equity.

> This largely reflects the significant allocation to foreign equity by the Australian superannuation industry together with the fact that the superannuation sector is relatively large as a share of the Australian economy.

This means Australian super funds own more offshore assets. Not a bad thing but not to be confused with lower reliance on foreign capital.

What Should the Objective Be?

Any government scheme requires clear objectives to remain focused and ultimately succeed.

Twenty-three years after the system commenced, the third Financial System Inquiry chaired by David Murray AO identified this problem and recommended an objective be established.

David Murray said:

> The superannuation system does not have a consistent set of policies that work towards common objectives. The absence of agreed objectives contributes to short-term ad hoc policy making. It adds complexity, imposes unnecessary costs on superannuation funds and their members, and undermines long-term confidence in the system.

Superannuation by its very nature is an inter-generational policy. Running it for almost a quarter of a century without an objective was irresponsible.

Murray's solution was simply to attach the system's existence to reduced pension outlays – by substitution or replacement.

This was adopted by the government which introduced legislation into Parliament in 2016 stating the objective was "to provide income in retirement to substitute or supplement the Age Pension."

At the time, the Parliament was unable to agree on an objective and we now approach 30 rudderless years without a clear objective.

The model Murray recommended is a good starting point. The system should be reducing pension outlays on a level greater than the cost. The super system should also pay for itself.

There are two significant costs to the system. One is the cost of the superannuation system to members which is $32 billion in fees charged.[8] This is more than Australians spend on power bills each year.[9]

The other cost is the tax concessions (to the taxpayer), principally driven by foregone income tax revenue, worth $36 billion annually.[10]

The $32 billion in fees and $36 billion fiscal cost of superannuation, should be taken into account when calculating the overall success of the system.

The Great Super Gap

The biggest issue facing Australians and their super is the "super gap". The great super gap is simply that most Australians will never be fully self-funded retirees.

Superannuation balances will not pay for retirement yet we have an enormous system which is constantly arguing how brilliant it is.

The average balance according to the industry is $196,400 for men and $129,100 for women at 45 years of age.

According to Rice Warner, $900,000 is required to fund a comfortable self-funded lifestyle in retirement, there is an enormous gap, especially for women.

Australians know about the gap. About thirty per cent of us

know the required balance is less than $1 million but more than $500,000. Another 16 per cent think it is between $1 and $2 million.

The 68 per cent pension reliance level, similarly blows away the myth that there will be legions of totally self-funded retirees and that there will be lower government expenditure on the pension.

A generation of governments and the super industry have created the expectation gap.

The gap needs to be addressed if the nation is to attain a 50 per cent self-funded target.

While the industry continues its myth making that everyone will be self-funded, Australians have a good sense of what is going on.

FIGURE 4: WILL YOU BE SELF-FUNDED IN RETIREMENT?

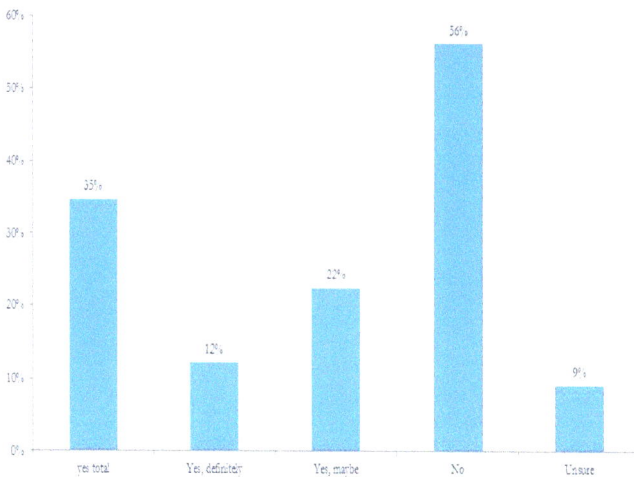

Source: EMRS

According to research undertaken for this monograph, just 12 per cent of Australians strongly believe they will be self-funded and another 22 per cent think they might be self-funded (34 per cent in total).

A large driver of the gap is a poor level of understanding about the level of contributions required to be fully self-funded.

In reality, middle income earners will need to save around 20 per cent of their pre-retirement earnings if they want to achieve self-sufficiency.

Rice Warner Actuaries say that a "range of 15 per cent to 20 per cent of salary" would be required.

The data in Figure 5 demonstrates the scale of the task to become fully self-funded.

FIGURE 5: ADEQUACY ATTAINMENT BY LEVEL OF SG - COUPLES (PER PERSON), 50TH INCOME DECILE, WITHOUT AGE PENSION

Source: Rice Warner

If the objective is to be self-funded, it is necessary to determine how we might achieve the objective.

"The how" goes to which cohorts require focus, how much ought to be saved, by what means and under which conditions. With a hugely disengaged population this will be challenging, the research shows that 25 per cent of people never check their super balance!

The initial mandatory contribution started at three per cent from 1 July 1992 with the Cabinet submissions of the day saying that super would reduce stress on the age pension. The long term plan was to get the contributions to 12 per cent by the year 2000.[11]

This contribution rose to 9 per cent by 2002 in increments legislated by the Keating Government which had been defeated in March 1996.

In a speech on "a retirement incomes policy" in July 1991, soon to be Prime Minister Paul Keating said:

> Unless we can move – and move rapidly – we will put the Commonwealth Government age pension system under unbearable stress and condemn an entire generation of elderly people to an unsatisfactory and poorly provided retirement.

These words require no translation. In his own words it "allows the aged to be more financially independent of the government."

Keating went on to say super "will make Australia a more equal place, a more egalitarian place and hence a more cohesive and happier place."

The one size fits all approach is bound up in the language of "universal application" of superannuation. Every Labor leader from Keating onward has used this language.

In a 2011 speech I remember well, former Prime Minister Julia Gillard said:

> Friends, superannuation used to be the preserve of the wealthy or of tenured public servants and academics. Universal super changed all that. Until universal superannuation came along, most Australians had one source of wealth – their home. With super, they can have two.

The one size fits all approach has failed for two reasons. Firstly, the industry has not been honest with Australians. It is clear that most middle income earners will never amass the super balance necessary to become self-funded retirees.

Secondly, lower income earners may be better served putting their money into other vehicles such as a home. This is an enormous trade off for lower income Australians.

As a general rule, a fundamental precondition to compel people to save is to avoid poverty.

The Centre for Independent Studies says one of the preconditions necessary to justify forced saving is that "under-saving for retirement will result in serious harm, including serious levels of old age poverty".

There is always going to be a large cohort of the community who will require a pension, thereby avoiding poverty, which the

OECD benchmarked at $35,060 per year for a couple.[12]

The notion that every single Australian regardless of income ought to make the exact same proportional contribution of their income ignores the way our social security system works.

A clear fiscal saving from super has not yet emerged. The industry (ASFA) assert the system is saving $9 billion per annum in reduced pension outlays which is a pittance.

The system is frighteningly expensive – $32 billion in fees charged by the industry and $36 billion in foregone tax revenue which is on top of $50 billion a year in Age Pension costs.

In arguing the case for the scheme's inception in 1991, Keating himself cited a study that suggested superannuation could reduce the pension reliance "from 77 to 65 per cent of the aged population by 2020."

Keating deserves praise for delivering, for the most part, what he promised. The current pension reliance is only 3 per cent higher than he promised. Sadly, the net cost of the scheme is stubbornly high. It costs more than it saves. As Brendan Coates of the Grattan Institute says "eventually – by 2050 – the net budgetary cost of super tax breaks will be 0.2 per cent of GDP a year....On these trends, superannuation won't start saving the budget money until about 2060 – and by then there will be 80 years of budget costs to pay back before government is in front." Translation: Super may never help the budget.

Given the significant budgetary cost of the scheme and the personal trade off consequences for lower income Australians, surely our ambition for super must be higher so there are more self-funded retirees. We should be aiming for at least 50 per cent of Australians to be independent in retirement.

12 per cent is not enough

Paul Keating's own nominated figure was never going to be sufficient to drive say 50 per cent of the populace into self-funding.

The Treasury recognised this in their 1992 'Security in Retirement' paper which estimates that the super guarantee would provide around 40 per cent of retirement income with another 40 per cent 'privately funded'.[13]

As Tilley said, the modelling was done on the "back of an envelope" which was lost so it is hardly a surprise that the numbers do not match.

Rice Warner Actuaries have shown that the 12 per cent mandatory super would not move pension reliance below the current 68 per cent. Even 15 per cent would equally fail to move the dial. Rice Warner says "(12 per cent super) will not have much impact on the Age Pension for many years," and the extra super tax breaks from higher compulsory super will cost an average of 0.22 per cent of GDP "throughout this century".

According to Rice Warner Actuaries, the required saving rate is as high as 20 per cent for an average worker.

This is the great super gap in action.

It is a gap borne of unmet expectations and unclear communication to the public over the past 30 years.

The calculations are based upon the long held assumption that Australians need 65 per cent of pre-retirement earnings. Rice Warner considers this a reasonable replacement rate for determining self-sufficiency in retirement.

It also assumes fees of around 0.8 per cent and earnings of around 6.7 per cent.[14] The issue is therefore clearly not about the mandatory rate.

It is about public communication of what super can realistically achieve for working Australians and driving a discussion on the value of voluntary savings.

Rather than pretending that a hypothetical 15 per cent mandatory contribution rate would make 55 per cent of Australians self-sufficient, which it will not, it would be far better to explain that 15 per cent gets you three quarters of the way there.

If more Australians knew they faced the super gap, I am certain there would be higher voluntary contributions amongst some cohorts.

For many Australians, salary sacrifice has been a popular scheme. Especially for workers that have finished paying a mortgage and school fees. Indeed, Australians made $7.5 billion in salary sacrifice contributions in 2018, which accounts for around 7 per cent of total superannuation contributions.[15]

To be self-funded, an average worker earning the median wage of $60,000 would need to top up their mandatory contribution of around $6,000 with another $6,000.

In years of child rearing, this is always going to be challenging which is why the system should provide more flexibility for Australians to provide "catch up" contributions.

The great super gap should be honestly addressed by the superannuation industry. Instead of hiding behind incomprehensible rhetoric about partial Age Pension savings, the sector should look to tell Australians the truth about the gap; and how to bridge it.

Some Australians take great pride in being completely self-funded and will strive to fill the gap. This is likely to be facilitated through salary sacrifice contributions which increase super contributions at a concessional tax rate.

To draw upon the median wage example again, a person who is given the bad news that their super contribution will only get them half way to a self-funded retirement, may be driven to salary sacrifice.

Others will be happy to have some super and some pension and will stop or slow reducing their take home pay. Being partly self-funded is a great personal objective, which should be celebrated, but it is not a replacement of the pension.

If properly furnished with the information, no doubt many Australians will stop putting voluntary contributions into super and instead save for a home deposit.

The more flexibility in the system to facilitate diverging

individual needs, the better.

4

THE BIG SUPER TRADE OFF

Would Australians be better off with super or with their hard earned money elsewhere, like a house?

Super is making home ownership so much harder for lower income Australians. Research by the Australian Research Council Centre of Excellence in Population Ageing Research has shown that 'the introduction of mandated super in 1992 may have crowded out housing investment, either early on in life, or indefinitely'.[1]

Since super started in 1992, every single age group below 65 has experienced lower levels of home ownership. Australia's decline in home ownership is fairly consistent amongst all age groups. Whilst many comparable western economies have faced a similar trend, none are as pronounced as Australia.

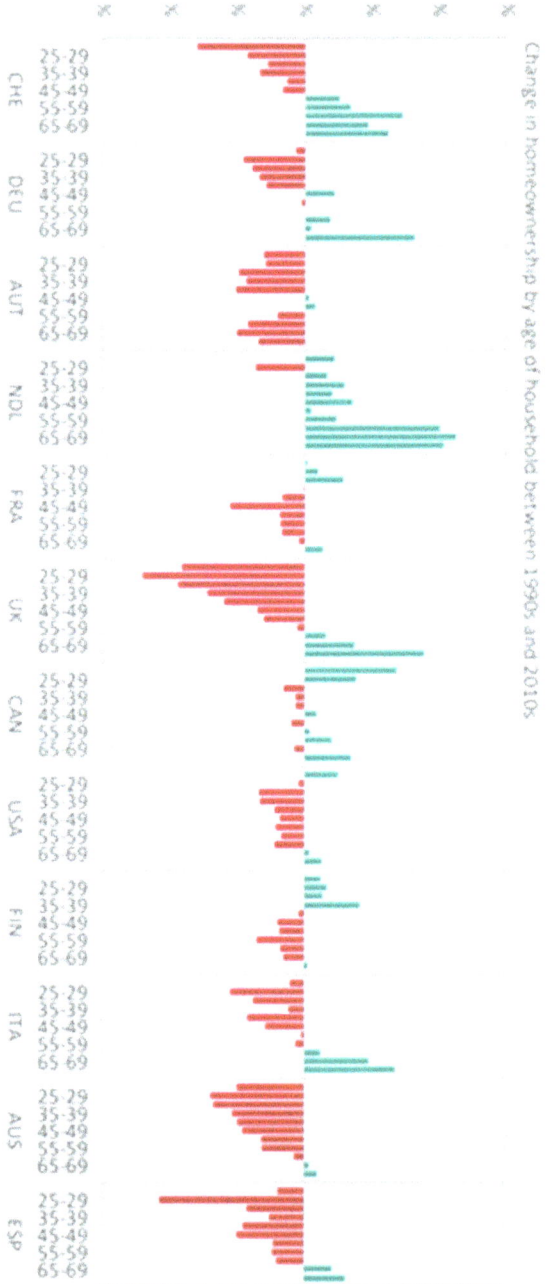

FIGURE 6: CHANGE IN HOMEOWNERSHIP BY AGE OF HOUSEHOLD BETWEEN THE 1990s AND 2010s.

Source: CEPAR research brief, November 2019

FIGURE 7: SUPER IS MAKING HOME OWNERSHIP SO MUCH HARDER

In 1996, 11% of 25-34 year olds owned their own household outright. By 2016, this number had dropped to 1.5%

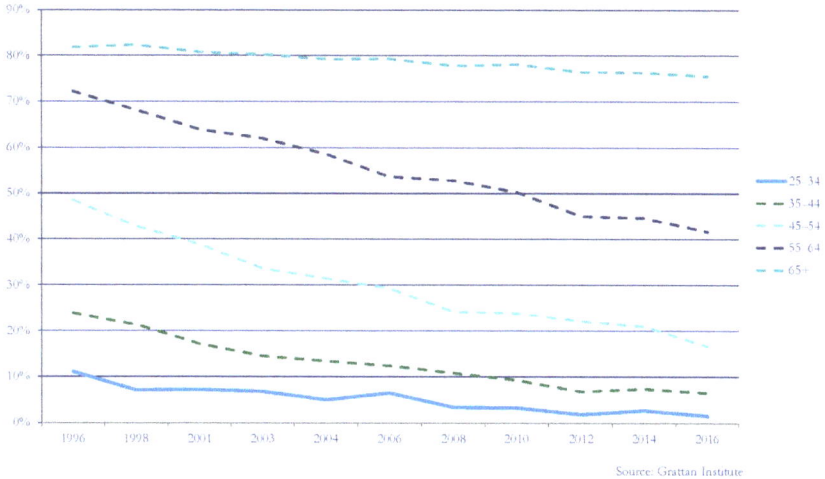

Source: Grattan Institute

Grattan Institute, 2019

The drop in home ownership has been particularly dramatic for young people. In 1996, outright home ownership was at 11.10 per cent for households between 25-34 of age. By 2016, outright home ownership had dropped to 1.50 per cent.[2]

The Centre for Independent Studies (CIS) found that the average deposit for a first home has doubled between 2000 and 2015.

The CIS says:

> The average deposit as a multiple of average earnings almost doubled between 2000 and 2015. And it is here that the interaction with compulsory super matters so much because as millennials are trying to save hundreds of thousands of dollars in order to get on

the bottom rung of the property ladder their income is docked nearly 10 per cent to save for their retirement.

There is little doubt that the massive increase in the deposit required to purchase a home substantially delays property ownership for first time buyers. This means that people will be older when they pay off their mortgage, in some cases substantially so. For some, this hurdle will never be overcome.

Superannuation, especially the increasing guarantee rate, makes that task harder still. In effect this means that, though it is likely that homeownership is more important than accumulating superannuation, the system prioritises superannuation above homeownership.

More Australians are struggling to buy a house and pay off their mortgage than ever. It was not always this hard. The median age to buy a first house in 1981 was 24; in 2011 it was 33. The median age to pay off mortgage in 1981 was 51; in 2011 it was 62.[3]

Australians, especially younger Australians, may well be better off with a home than super.

In the *Financial Planning Research Journal* in the article entitled 'Averting Poverty and Government Budgetary Pressure Through Releasing Home Equity: A Safe and Informed Solution for Baby Boomer Home Owners' shows that purchasing a home at the age of 30 can lead to over $500,000 in additional home equity than purchasing one at the age of 65.

FIGURE 8: AVERAGE SIMULATED WEALTH AT RETIREMENT BY AGE OF HOME PURCHASE, BY ASSET, SUPER, LIQUID ASSETS, AND HOME EQUITY.

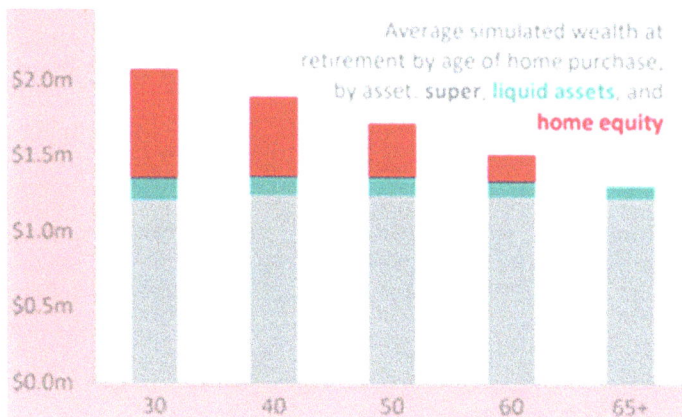

CEPAR research brief, November 2019

A house offers significant financial flexibility to people. Through downsizing or reverse mortgage, the family home can be a useful means to save for a rainy day.

Without a house, people suffer financially.

Renters face significantly more financial distress than homeowners. In a study conducted by the Grattan Institute, 41.35 per cent of renters who are on welfare between the ages of 18 and 65 faced at least one financial stress. In comparison, only 14.75 per cent of homeowners who are on welfare experienced financial stress.[4]

Financial stress is defined as whether; due to a money shortage, a household - 1) skipped meals; 2) did not heat their home; 3) failed to pay gas 4) failed to pay registration insurance.

A particularly concerning trend is that despite the increase in life expectancy, there has been a decrease in home ownership. This trend 'could see higher expenses in retirement and an increase in longevity risk for individuals' according to the Retirement Income Review conducted by the Treasury.[5]

Indeed, retired renters are much more likely to experience poverty than homeowners. Forty-two per cent of retired renters face poverty compared to 6 per cent for homeowners.[6]

FIGURE 9: OLD-AGE POVERTY RATE AFTER INCLUDING IMPUTED RENT, AGES 65+

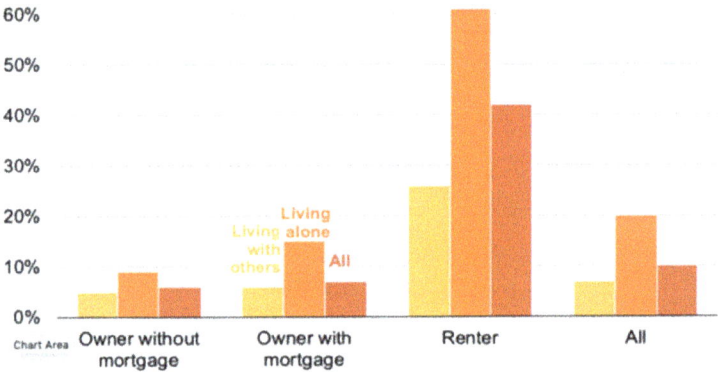

Source: Grattan Institute

While I will avoid providing portfolio construction advice at all costs, there are irrefutable advantages to owning a home.

As Bird, Hu and Hulley of UNSW say "allowing low income households to access their super balance to acquire their first home increases their welfare by in excess of 25 per cent; home ownership is more effective than super in contributing to the lifetime welfare of low income households."

I am not solely referring to financial advantages. Homes are spaces and places where memories can be created.

A drive for home ownership amongst Australia's working people has been a feature of Liberal Party policy for 75 years.

Menzies made home ownership a cornerstone and even discussed it in his earlier Forgotten People broadcasts.

Our commitment to home ownership extends to the present day. The government has looked to innovative ways to unlock home ownership.

As stated by the ATO, from 2018 the First Home Super Saver Scheme has allowed prospective first home buyers to save for a deposit for a home through their super. Hundreds of people have used this scheme to pull together an elusive deposit.

This scheme provides that voluntary contributions can be used for a first home deposit.

ATO data has shown that in the first 16 months of operation, 7,016 individuals have requested $90 million to be released from their super under this scheme.

Out of this, the ATO has released $70.5 million to 5,622 individuals. There has been a 90 per cent increase in the number of requests compared to the same time the previous financial year.

There is no reason this scheme couldn't be expanded so that compulsory contributions could also be used for a first home, thereby removing the trade off.

The super system should not prevent people from buying a home. Certainly, Australians should be able to select where their savings go if their ambition is to purchase a house.

According to the research commissioned for this monograph, 63 per cent of Australians say they would like to access their super for a first home deposit.

FIGURE 10: IS IT A GOOD IDEA TO ALLOW SUPER FOR A FIRST HOME?

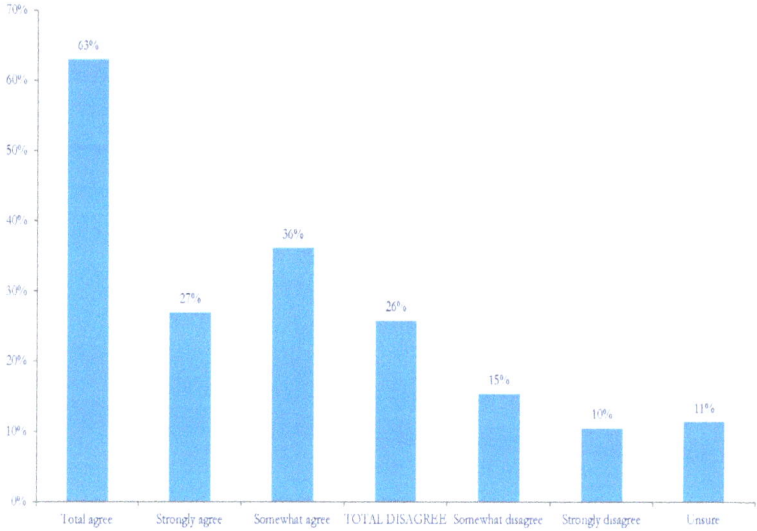

Source:: EMRS

5

WHO ACTUALLY PAYS

An important part of the trade off discussion is who actually pays for super.

Much has been made of the payment of superannuation by employers. Or is it by employees? Super is actually a cost of employment which is borne by employees. Even the superannuation industry admits super is "deferred wages". Yet it remains confusing and the confusion pollutes the debate.

The inception of the scheme was part of the accord process between the Hawke Labor Government and the trade union movement. The initial contribution of three per cent was in lieu of a pay rise so it was clear that the workers paid the super; into a super fund, not a bank account.

It was clear that employees pay for their super. This has been the consistent finding of groups such as the Australian Council of Social Services, Centre for Independent Studies and Grattan. The Reserve Bank of Australia has also lowered its wage forecasts due to the proposed increase in the superannuation guarantee saying that an SG increase "shaved" wages growth.

Future enterprise agreements are already taking the proposed higher SG into account by reducing take home pay.

There is a misnomer that super is paid by employers which has been amplified by the super industry through its public relations juggernaut.

The reality is that private sector roles regularly provide a consolidated salary including super. It is not broken down because super is a cost of employment, paid by the employer, but borne by the worker. This is supported by simple desktop research. In early 2020, out of 100 employment adverts, 82 adverts had no mention of super. This demonstrates that super is bundled.

Government salaries do not generally include super when quoted. Accordingly, it could be credibly argued that in the case of public servants, super is paid by the employer.

I am a member of the Commonwealth Parliament. My salary is set out separately to the superannuation guarantee contribution of 15.4 per cent. Even at 15.4 per cent, it is unlikely that I would be totally free of a pension payment in retirement.

The mechanics of making the contributions has troubled small business since the inception of the scheme.

As the Council of Small Business of Australia Chief Executive Peter Strong says, "we are the only people who don't get paid." By that Strong means the super industry and the employees are both paid but the small businessperson is not remunerated for their time navigating the super contribution maze.

The cost of small business providing mandatory superannuation administration services is estimated to cost small business close to $1 billion dollars each year according to COSBOA.

The problem with the pervasive perception that employers pay super for private sector workers is that it further entrenches a view that the government has solved the retirement problem. It fosters a "she'll be right" culture on retirement planning as it makes super even more removed from people's daily lives.

Research for this monograph shows the community is very unsure. 41 per cent say their employer pays super, 22 per cent say it is paid by themselves, 5 per cent say it's the government, 23 per cent say all of the above and 9 per cent are unsure.

"Who pays" is yet another dark cobweb on a confusing system.

FIGURE 11: WHO PAYS YOUR SUPER?

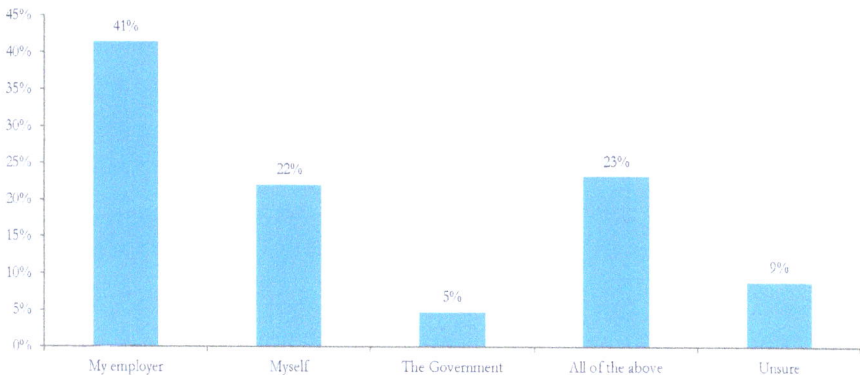

Source: EMRS

Engagement Levels

The 'employer pays' mythology contributes to the great super gap. It drives disengagement which remains high despite super being the second largest asset for most Australians and increasingly the largest as home ownership levels fall.

FIGURE 12: HOW OFTEN DO YOU CHECK YOUR SUPER BALANCE?

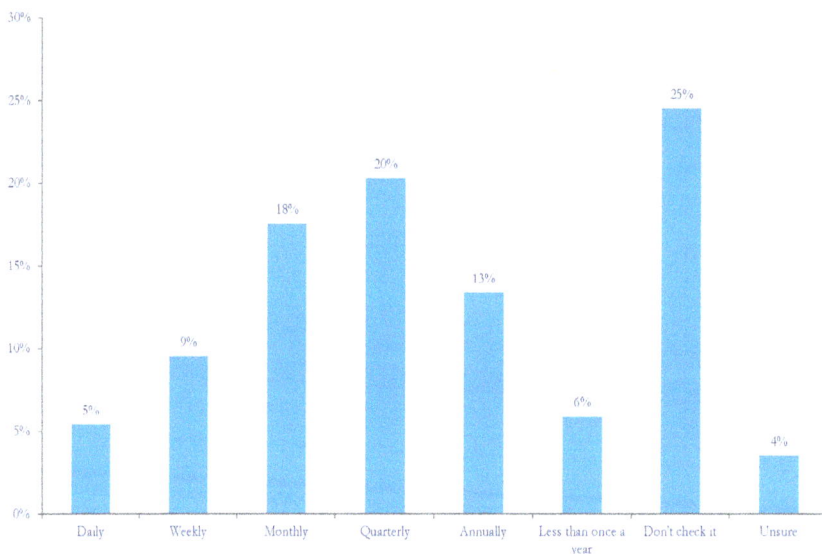

Source: EMRS

Only 7 per cent of Australians are actively engaged and well-informed about superannuation according to the Productivity Commission.[1] Research commissioned for this book shows 25 per cent of all Australians don't check their super balance.

Even fewer change funds with annual fund switching rates varying between 2 per cent - 10 per cent, half of which can be attributed to changing jobs.[2] The truth is, many Australians are forbidden from choosing their own fund because of a loophole in the 2005 choice of fund legislation.

This loophole has been ruthlessly exploited by unions and businesses through enterprise agreements which remove choice of fund rights.

The system has been designed by the industry to foster disengagement. Following a Productivity Commission recommendation, the Coalition government decided to make life insurance 'opt in' for people under 25 years.

To overcome the great super gap, baseline engagement levels and comprehension of the system will have to increase markedly.

Without better engagement and understanding, the system is destined to deliver just 30 per cent of Australians as self-funded retirees regardless of the compulsory rate of Superannuation Guarantee.

Thankfully Australia is not a European state which could contemplate compulsory contributions at and above 20 per cent.

We are far too dynamic to require that form of intervention. No Australian government has seriously proposed or even discussed mandatory super contributions above 15 per cent.

Even if they did, the system would still yield just 30 per cent of the populace being self-funded. The great super gap cannot therefore be solved by the government.

The only solution to the great super gap is more engagement.

6

A 1980s SYSTEM

With the objectives and required contribution a bit clearer, the next question is scheme design.

The scheme was designed in an age where more homogeneity was a feature of the Australian workplace. More Australians worked 9-5 hours a day at larger businesses.

With the rise of the 'gig economy' a significant amount of Australians now make money through platforms such as Uber, AirBnB and Airtasker.

This is especially pronounced in the lower age groups where up to 20 per cent of Australians between ages 18-34 have earned money by working or offering services through digital platforms.

Whilst only 5.4 per cent of gig economy workers work more than 26 hours a week, nearly 20 per cent of these workers earned half their income via digital platforms.[1]

Many Australians rely on digital platforms to live.

Such statistics would have been unimaginable and certainly unforeseeable when the super system was conceived in the 1990s.

There are many consequences of the 1980s workforce design being maintained in 2020 which include:

1. Super is not generally paid on flexible work in the gig economy;
2. Self-employed Australians generally don't have super despite a specific regime existing to incentivise self-employed to establish super accounts;
3. Lower income earners find it harder to purchase a home;
4. Australians working later in life can find it difficult to contribute to super.

These are but a few examples where retirement income pillars do not apply as simply as they would have 30 years ago in a fairly static working environment.

More flexibility in the system would surely improve the outcomes for members.

Another system feature is sustained intra-industry conflict.

Whilst the Commonwealth legislates for a single set of rules for public offer super funds, the industry often behaves like warring tribes.

A Culture War

A culture of introspection within the super industry has created a culture war.

The constant public bickering and squabbling between the two major super industry service providers is unique to industry generally in Australia, and within the super and funds management industry globally it is extremely difficult to find instances of such internecine conflict.

The damage such activity does to the public confidence in the super system is incalculable.

Super funds in Australia are clearly focused on internal constituencies – often financial sector conglomerates or unions.

The funds participation in civil wars has been a prominent feature of significant advertising campaigns.

I spent part of my pre-Parliamentary career participating in this civil war.

I can now see how unproductive this activity was compared with focusing on outcomes for savers.

There remain many questions on fund transparency but these are secondary compared to outcomes for savers.

The industry should set the civil war aside because the effectiveness of the whole system is the only thing that matters to policy makers. It should take the long view, the national interest view.

As I outlined in my First Speech to Parliament:

> We do not stand for any business or any vested interest.
>
> As Menzies himself said, we stand for the Forgotten People –
> the great Australian middle class. They were (in his words) 'the
> salary earners, shopkeepers, skilled artisans, professional men
> and women.'
>
> We support enterprise. We believe in markets. And we believe
> in some regulation of industry. We believe markets must serve
> the public interest.

I have no interest in participating in the super culture war.

Certainly the electors of New South Wales expect that I take
my own advice and focus on the interests of the electorate as
a whole.

Accordingly, the whole industry, not industry sectors, should
always be the focus of members of Parliament.

The forgotten people have no interest in wars between highly
superannuated tribes. I reflected on this deeply when I was
drafting my First Speech. I read Deakin, Menzies and Theodore
Roosevelt.

We on the centre-right have a fine tradition of being the workers'
champion – a culture war would undermine our capacity to be
that champion. This does not mean we shy away from pointing
out failings inside bank or union controlled super funds.

Menzies created the Liberal Party to work for workers.

Ultimately, the class war is a fool's war. The idea that super funds represented by industry wide labels are homogenous is actually untrue. There is little in common between the largest and smallest industry or retail fund.

That is a discussion for another day but the fact remains, if the culture war continues; only the system suffers.

I am institutionally critical of the industry super funds as they operate in a political block to support the Labor Party in a way that no other sector of the business community operates. The barracking industry super performed for the Labor Party in the 2019 election well and truly demonstrates their partisanship.

This does not mean I am a supporter of any other particular group of funds. I am a critic of the conflicted, poorly performing, poorly governed retail funds which committed gross misdeeds, which were uncovered by Kenneth Hayne's Royal Commission.

Key System Features

It is clear that fees and costs have a significant drag on retirement incomes which is why governments of all shades have sought lower super fees.

The Rice Warner modelling used throughout this short book includes a notional fee of 0.8 per cent of the account balance in the accumulation phase and 1 per cent in the retirement phase.[46]

There is still much room for getting fees down through stronger competitive tensions and a more consumer focused market structure.

Beyond headline fees, there are many scheme design features which impact the effectiveness of super.

1. Choice and market design
2. Fees and costs regulation
3. Insurance
4. Tax

The next two chapters address these issues in greater detail.

7

NO CHOICE,
NO COMPETITION

Much has been made of the superannuation scheme being of the labour movement which is a justification for super being embedded into industrial relations institutions.

Certainly, super has continued to pay handsome dividends to the two principal groups present at its legal foundations in the late 1980s and early 1990s: employer groups and unions.

Employer groups and unions partnered to create super funds for various segments of the economy. They have collectively received significant distributions thereafter.

For example, the CBUS fund has a board controlled by the Master Builders Association and the CFMMEU. This fund has paid the CFMMEU $14.5 million in the past few years. These payments are not disclosed to members in annual reports or websites.[1]

Default funds

In the 1990s one of the key design features was the establishment of "default funds", as under the new compulsory system, it was envisioned that Australians would be ambivalent.

Whilst some state and federal awards hard coded a particular superannuation fund, in most cases, a complying fund would be sufficient.

John Howard's government established a programme of "award modernisation" which was destined to consolidate hundreds of state and federal awards down to 122 modern awards which would apply across the economy.

This was only possible after the states referred their industrial relations power to the Commonwealth.

The Howard Government lost office part way through the award modernisation process. The Rudd government's Minister for Superannuation Nick Sherry wrote to the then Australian Industrial Relations Commission with a specific request. Sherry asked the AIRC to enshrine superannuation funds as "default funds" in the new modern awards as agreed by unions and employer groups.

The AIRC dutifully established default funds in most of the 122 modern awards based on applications from the two groups. The results were not a surprise given the vested interests at play.

The CFMMEU and Master Builders collectively own CBUS and unsurprisingly nominated CBUS which was adopted by the AIRC.

This conflicted process allowed unions and employers to impose any type of super fund upon workers – regardless of its fees, services and insurance. The only prerequisite was, "is this our fund?"

Unless an employer had been using a different fund prior to 2008, the funds prescribed in the modern awards would become compulsory for employers with award reliant workers.

This created an enormously anti-competitive market structure where industrial connections established protected markets for related party super funds.

At the time, the Labor Government initiated a review headed by former ASIC deputy Jeremy Cooper. Cooper found only 20 per cent of Australians choose their own fund.[2] This meant the conferring of default status was the equivalent to awarding a sheep station to a farmer.

This opaque process was not well understood or widely profiled. Until the global financial crisis of 2008-09, superannuation did not regularly make the front page. Superannuation was not yet a vote changer as it would be in each of the 2013, 2016 and 2019 general elections.

The AIRC's deal with the Industrial Relations (IR) club, sanctioned by the Rudd government came to light with a front page story in the Financial Review by chief political correspondent David Crowe during 2011.

The headline "Union pushed workers into super loser" profiled the story of one of the worst performing funds in the crisis being recommended and endorsed as a default fund in the wide ranging General Retail Industry Award 2010.

Crowe's work demonstrated consumers had clearly been put last:

> The Australian Financial Review reported yesterday that the Australian Manufacturing Workers Union applied successfully to add the MTAA Superannuation Fund to six industrial awards covering hundreds of thousands of workers, giving the fund access to a valuable stream of super contributions.
>
> The AMWU lodged the requests despite a steep decline in the MTAA fund's performance in recent years and without declaring that the two union officials making the applications, Ian Jones and Alix Sachinidis, were also trustees of the fund.[3]

This and subsequent stories meant the opaqueness melted away and the process was now well understood. Eventually the Productivity Commission would be tasked with reviewing the system. It recommended significant changes as the lack of competitive tensions were undermining consumer outcomes.

In effect, the PC recommended abolishing the secretive process and replacing it with a transparent application process with Ministerial appointments drawn from people with relevant experience and expertise. This process would be run by an "expert panel".

The PC recommended busting open the system: "The selection of default products for awards should be merit rather than precedent based, and should encourage improved performance through competition."

The review was adopted in part by the Gillard Government under which Superannuation Minister Bill Shorten decided to materially depart from the process recommended by the PC.

Shorten entrenched default super inside the successor body to the AIRC, Gillard's Fair Work Commission.

Shorten's design, conceived somewhere other than Treasury, the Department of Employment and the Productivity Commission, meant the full bench of the Fair Work Commission would be involved in determining default superannuation funds. This is despite the PC finding the full bench had no expertise in this field.

This process was legislated in 2013.

Sadly for its architects, the Shorten process has never seen the light of day. During 2015, my employer at the time, the Financial Services Council, which had been hostile to the Shorten model decided to challenge the eligibility of members of the expert panel.

The President of the Commission, Iain Ross made a number of moves to ensure the FWC could complete the Shorten process. This is the same Iain Ross of ACTU fame, who according to Bill Kelty, was the brains behind the establishment of the superannuation scheme.

The FSC took the Fair Work Commission to the Full Bench of the Federal Court to stop Ross and challenge the eligibility of expert panel members whom were believed to be conflicted.

The FSC won this case. However, it meant the funds listed in the awards and those in use prior to 2008 continue to enjoy a significant market advantage.

The system put in place by Rudd, Gillard and Sherry lives on.

The way in which default funds are selected has been considered by various PC reviews. It will continue to be an issue of industry consternation because the selection process or formula directly impacts funds under management. In essence, it is the distribution component.

The interests that stand to benefit to the tune of more than $10 billion in automatic contributions a year will spend big to defend the system.

Equally, the funds that do not have a share of guaranteed Fair Work allocations will spend up to advance an open door policy.

This is a unique market: a compulsory savings system built into compulsory industrial relation awards which has survived virtually intact since 1992.

When asked to look at the system again, the Productivity Commission made some grim findings.

In 2019 the PC found:

> Australia's super system needs to adapt to better meet the needs of a modern workforce and a growing pool of retirees. Structural flaws – unintended multiple accounts and entrenched under

performers are harming millions of members, and regressively so.

Fixing these twin problems could benefit members to the tune of $3.8 billion each year. Even a 55 year old today could gain $79 000 by retirement. A new job entrant today would have $533 000 more when they retire in 2064.

The lack of dynamism, competition and proliferation of unnecessary new accounts must be addressed in the medium term.

A government backstop

One of the longer term solutions which has been floated to address the market issues in default super has been to expand the Future Fund's mandate to accept default contributions.

The Future Fund was created to manage public sector superannuation liabilities. The defined benefit schemes of yesteryear had the potential to eat the Federal Budget unless provisions were made for the enormous liabilities.

Accordingly, Treasurer Peter Costello in the Howard Government created it and used Telstra sale proceeds to ensure the fund could get to scale.

Standing at over $150 billion, the fund has performed well over its life.[4]

The Future Fund stands as a great but undersold achievement of Australian liberalism. Rather than being crippled by defined benefit liabilities from the enormous public service, we have a sovereign wealth fund which protects the budget.

Costello is often said to be the best Treasurer Australia has had. I think this is a fair judgement. Over 12 budgets, Costello paid down $96 billion of Labor's debt, delivered significant personal and company tax cuts and established the Future Fund.[5]

Over the past 10 years (according to Chant West in 2019) the average super fund has returned 8.8 per cent a year on average. The Future Fund has returned 10 per cent a year on average over 10 years.[6]

This is a complicated comparison for a number of reasons. Super funds pay tax whereas the Future Fund does not. Equally there are liquidity and mandate differences which mean it is not an apples with apples comparison. Chant West says: "Clearly it is not valid to just compare this return to the Future Fund return since tax is payable in super funds but not in the Future Fund."

However super funds receive mandated and ongoing contribution flows and often perform very poorly compared to the Future Fund when including performance with or without tax.

For example, over the past five years Maritime Super delivered returns of 6.2 per cent, TWU delivered 7.6 per cent, REST super delivered 7.4 per cent, MLC delivered 7.9 per cent, Mercer delivered 7.5 per cent, IOOF delivered 7.9 per cent and Prime Super delivered 8.53 per cent. With or without tax, they are a long way behind the Future Fund.[7]

TABLE 3: HISTORICAL FUND PERFORMANCE DATA

Fund	Type	5 Year Net Investment Return (Single Strategy)
MLC	Retail	7.9%
Mercer	Retail	7.5%
IOOF	Retail	7.9%
PRIME	Retail	8.53%
TWU	Industry	7.6%
REST	Industry	7.4%
MARITIME	Industry	6.2%

Source: APRA Data

The Future Fund has not received a contribution for almost 15 years. It has not received a cent from government.

A semi-government default fund with a low fee mandate could work. They are widely used in other jurisdictions which have even stronger pro-market instincts than Australian policymakers.

As the Wall Street journal reports, the Nevada Public Employees Retirement Fund " commands funds whose returns over one-year, three-year, five-year and 10-year periods ending June 30 bested the nation's largest public pension, the California Public Employees' Retirement System, or Calpers, and deeply-staffed plans of many other states.

A fund with higher fees does not mean higher returns. The Nevada fund demonstrates this in practice. If it "consumed a typical Wall Street diet, it would pay roughly $120 million in annual fees. In 2016, Nevada paid $18 million."[8]

The low fee government backstop should be considered. The Future Fund could play a broader role in superannuation but not in the way it has been presented publicly in recent years.

The Future Fund could not be a "retail" operator. It is not equipped to deal with the public much like the Rudd Government discovered that the Commonwealth is not very good at putting pink batts into roofs.

Accordingly, the Future Fund could play a critical role in super but only as a wholesale fund manager supplying a government public fund.

For example, the Commonwealth could establish a trustee called "Super Guarantee Australia" (SGA). This trustee would be the default fund for all workers who fail to select a super fund. Its low fee mandate would drive the industry's $32 billion in annual fees down to a more reasonable level.

SGA would then outsource management of its assets to various fund managers including the Future Fund.

This way, retail consumers get access to the well-managed, top performing Future Fund without compromising the highly successful structure underpinning the Fund's success.

This approach would enact the recommendations of the 1976

Hancock Review into National Superannuation which was ignored by the Hawke/Keating Governments which gifted management of super to unions and retail funds.

Enterprise agreements

In 2005, the Howard government delivered choice of super fund to Australians.

Opposed by the Labor Party, choice of fund was supposed to guarantee that workers could select a complying fund other than the workplace default fund.

The pull of the players benefiting from the default fund system no doubt influenced Labor's long-standing opposition. Super choice was delivered through a deal with Senate cross-benchers.

In the horse trading, the final bill included a carve out whereby enterprise agreements could revoke choice of fund rights where certain conditions were met.

In the decade and a half since, unions and employers have ruthlessly exploited the loophole to take away choice rights.

This has been particularly prevalent in the retail trading industry where a determined effort has been underway to relieve workers of their opportunities.

The way it works is, Australia has laws which are supposed to guarantee that workers get to choose their own super fund.

Yet the laws work in a way which allows businesses to agree an "enterprise agreement" that makes one super fund compulsory for all workers in a single workplace or business.

In these agreements, there is no way for workers to change to a different fund. Choice is banned.

Clearly this is wrong. Given it's a compulsory system and the range of products is so diverse in terms of features, fees and performance, denial of a right to choose is outrageous.

That is why the Morrison Government is committed to ensuring all Australians can choose their own super fund.

It's hard to believe this is even an issue in 2020. It has been made easier to choose a bank or an energy provider in recent years yet this "rort" is more entrenched than ever.

There are too often well concealed reasons prior attempts to move on this issue have been stymied.

First, big business is part of the problem.

As someone who has worked in "big business", it has shocked me how business has become complicit in anti-worker conduct.

These secret deals to steal workers' rights can only happen if big business agrees. Unions cannot do it without being in bed with bosses.

How can big business call for economic reform and simultaneously stand by this rot?

One outrageous example is a Toll Holdings agreement which bans workers from choosing their own fund.

This deal was examined by the Trade Union Royal Commission. It emerged Toll truck driver Paul Bracegirdle tried to pick a fund other than TWU Super to boost his savings to provide for his daughter.

Bracegirdle's request was legally denied and he was told by a union official to "f**k off, no one cares Paul. Go away."

Yet Labor has defended the unholy alliance of big business and big unions screwing workers out of personal choices.

One of Labor's economic team members Andrew Leigh initially said that Labor didn't know what to think about a proposal to allow people to choose: "Labor will reserve our position on these proposed choice of fund changes until the Senate committee has reported."

The Labor Senators subsequently found choice was not okay:

> As part of these negotiations between employers and employees, many industries determined that there would be benefits to both employers and employees in having all employees contribute to a single fund, often an industry fund.

Translation: competition is bad.

Worse still Labor Senators said:

> Superannuation remains an evolving industry, and Labor Senators believe that careful consideration should be given to

how opening up choice of fund might preclude other innovative product offerings if the risk pooling of membership cannot be achieved.

Translation: less competition will promote innovation! This would make the Soviets smile.

Second, the rationale for enterprise agreements stealing choice of fund rights is superficial. Worse, it is anti-competitiveness cloaked in consumer-protection speak.

The standard argument against change is that workers may not get the same benefits away from the "mandatory" fund.

In some cases, that may actually happen, but it's certainly no justification for banning choice.

The arguments against Australians choosing a super fund cannot be sustained on any consumer basis. The existing laws certainly benefit big unions, big business and the finance sector. They live Lang's credo when it comes to compulsory super and maintaining it in its present form.

Overall, if the market had wholesale and retail competitive tensions in play with a government backstop, the fees payable by members would be lower; just as the service offering would increase.

Market competition is not outside the realm of possibility.

The Morrison Government has delivered the architecture for an "open banking" regime which will allow consumers to access the benefits of competition in banking. In time this mechanism will be extended to energy and telecommunications.

Super is arguably an easier market because it is both compulsory and features more heavy consumer focused regulation than the other markets.

An "open super" model is a highly desirable objective just as it is critical to sweep away barriers to people choosing their own super fund.

8

THE KIT AND CABOODLE

Fees and Costs

The fees in the superannuation scheme have been subject to various regulatory initiatives over the lifespan of compulsory super.

The bulk of regulatory initiatives focused on better disclosure until the advent of the "MySuper" reforms of 2012.

The system's fees exceed $32 billion per annum, so there should be plenty of scrutiny.

MySuper was the solution proposed by Jeremy Cooper during his 2009-10 Super System review of the scheme instead of fee caps or more disclosure.

Cooper's basis for recommending MySuper was that there ought to be a set of basic standards attached to a default super product. The primary objective would be to drive fees down.

By standardising features and aiding simplicity and comparability, fees would be driven down.

One component of the MySuper reforms included defining fees and the disclosure thereof. For example, there would be a definition of what an administration fee was, in terms of what type of activities it includes.

An administration fee might include providing a call centre whereas an investment fee may contain costs associated with asset management or consulting.

The idea behind MySuper is that comparability will drive more engagement and more member choice.

Yet attempts to increase the disclosure requirements of superannuation funds has not been wholly successful. The PC identified that 25 per cent of funds did not report any investment expenses to APRA in 2016 or 2017. Furthermore, an estimated $7 billion administrative and investment fees were not reported to APRA in 2017.[1]

More transparency for members should be provided, especially in relation to the default product.

During a 2019 Parliamentary Joint Committee on Corporations and Financial Services hearing, ASIC confirmed to me that superannuation funds do not have to tell their members if they use customers' funds to pay fines imposed by the regulator.

A compulsory savings system requires no less than full disclosure.

Disclosure requirements should be especially stringent in the context of not-for-profit super funds such as industry and public sector funds as the fines are paid from member's accounts or the funds' reserves.

Hostplus was fined $12,000 by ASIC for misleading members that they were offering 'independent advice' when in fact the advisors were employed by a company part-owned by Hostplus.[2] Media Super was fined $10,000 for providing misleading information when comparing itself to other funds.[3]

These fines were not adequately disclosed to members.

Insurance

Insurance is the ultimate "bell and whistle".

Like so many other components of the superannuation scheme, life insurance inside super was designed as a "one size fits all". This has led many Australians to have insurance they do not need.

As late as 2012, when the MySuper reforms were legislated, it was felt appropriate to guarantee all default members have essentially the same death and total and permanent disability insurance.

Compulsory life insurance inside superannuation is not working for all Australians. That is the view of the Productivity Commission, Choice and the Consumer Action Law Centre.

The arguments against changing insurance – that vulnerable people will be uninsured and workers in high-risk jobs won't have coverage in the event of a permanent disability – have been run by the vested interests: unions, Labor and parts of the finance industry.

Indeed, multiple reports have found compulsory life insurance is actually working for the insurance industry, not Australians.

If you listen to those who stand to benefit most from current arrangements, you could be forgiven for thinking the world will come to an end if changes are made.

Take super fund REST, which proclaims: "The burden will fall on government to provide financial support and services for those members who suffered a disability and did not receive any insurance."

Translation: Australians are too ignorant to acquire insurance on an 'opt in' basis.

Here's how it worked until late 2019: if you are working, you have a super fund and you have life insurance unless you 'opt out' of the system. It doesn't matter how young you are or how much money you have in your account.

This means that a 20-year-old without dependents or debts has life insurance that eats away at their accumulated savings. The Productivity Commission says these excess insurance premiums cost savers $1.9 billion per annum.[2]

The PC recommended: "Insurance should be made opt in for members aged under 25 (rather than opt out, as is currently the case)."

There are two reasons why this law was enacted by the Coalition.

First, the system was unfair.

If you are young, you probably don't need insurance. Consumer group Choice (not exactly a bastion of right-wing ideologues) says that "for most under 25s life insurance, particularly death cover, will offer little to no value".

If you're a lower income worker, you will pay for this system. The PC found that "balance erosion for low-income members due to insurance could reach a projected 14 per cent of retirement balances in many cases, and in extreme cases (for low-income members with intermittent work patterns and with multiple income protection policies) could be well over a quarter of a member's retirement balance".

The "balance erosion" refers to an industry practice of taking out premiums whether or not people are working, often for insurance which is poorly targeted.

There are cases where people have seen $50,000 of their super disappear due to zombie insurance policies.

It is also unfair because it encourages a "she'll be right" mentality, which is most likely to hurt people with lower levels of financial literacy.

Government and insurers cannot foresee people's insurance needs. Most insurance in super policies will pay out between $100,000 and $200,000 in death benefits. But in reality, full-time workers with young children should have around $600,000 in insurance coverage according to Rice Warner Actuaries.

That is a big gap.

This "one size fits all" approach discourages Australians from seeking proper advice about the insurance coverage they actually need for their own circumstances. This analysis would take into account a person's family situation, income, objectives and risks.

Second, it undermines the purpose of super. The Murray estimation of super proposes achieving a simple outcome: reduce the public sector costs of an ageing population.

This objective depends on a superannuation system which is efficient and fit for purpose: not one with unnecessary fees and costs.

Insurance is one of many factors undermining this system of national savings. Again to the PC report:

> The effect on age pension outlays of the erosion of superannuation balances by insurance premiums is not trivial, and could materially offset any savings to government in social security outlays (that would otherwise have been paid to members that become insurance payout recipients).

In other words, poorly targeted insurance is working against the objectives of super.

The most recent Intergenerational Report estimated that at the current rate, most Australians are still on track to require some form of pension by mid-century.

To get more people off the Age Pension, we need higher super balances, not poorly targeted insurance policies draining their savings.

A 2019 Senate Inquiry into a life insurance in super bill provides an example of how the current system fails to advocate for members.

Of the 46 Inquiry submissions, 70 per cent argue the system is basically working well.

These respondents benefit from the current system and fail to address the fact that unnecessary insurance drains $1.9 billion from super each year.

Legislation to close the insurance gravy train passed Parliament in late 2019. Insurance is an add on element of the super scheme, so we should continue to search for refinements to get workers a better deal on their super.

The compulsion of the scheme compels us to endlessly search for a better deal for workers.

Tax

Tax is another significant drag on retirement savings. The scheme as created by Keating contributed to the ever pressing need to balance a budget. The tax system for super was designed during a period of sustained budget pressure.

Too many broader tax, revenue and budget factors have driven taxation changes to super in the past two decades.

It began with the initial design. Australia's superannuation scheme does not follow a typical taxation approach. Instead we adopted a novel framework for taxation. This reversed the normal method of maintaining a lower taxation burden on the savings at the beginning of the saving period.

This allowed the government of the day to maximise tax revenues in the here and now. Unfortunately this model removes a large benefit of the overseas model which is generating the maximum amount of compound earnings.

Superannuation provides a strong tax incentive for most working Australians.

Before the Howard Government reformed superannuation taxation, the super tax scheme was actually tax, tax and tax.

The 15 per cent contributions tax applies for workers between $0 and $250,000. The same workers then face a 15 per cent earnings tax.

Until the Howard Government abolished taxes on the drawdown phase in 2007, there were also taxes on the way out depending on the superannuation arrangement.

The Turnbull Government subsequently put in place a tax free cap of $1.6 million (non-indexed) per person which means a couple could have $3.2 million tax free in a super pension account.

Under this tax system, the government collects more revenue and savers benefit less from the benefit of compound earnings.

Yet superannuation tax concessions remain enormous at $36 billion and growing. As Treasury says in its 2019 Retirement Income Review:

> Superannuation earnings attract the largest superannuation-

related tax concession in dollar terms, closely followed by employer superannuation contributions. The revenue forgone as a result of superannuation tax concessions is expected to continue to grow as the superannuation system matures.

The review rightly asks a number of questions on system sustainability. Successive governments have made piecemeal changes to the superannuation scheme outside of a long term framework which the Retirement Income Review now provides.

At a minimum, the system should pay for itself. In other words, lower pension outlays should exceed the tax concessions required to run the system.

9

IDEAS TO IMPROVE SUPER

The point of this monograph is to remind the nation what we are trying to achieve with super and how we are tracking against that objective.

If we are to recalibrate the system, we should be guided by the evidence at hand which in summary tells us the system should work harder for the investment we make in it.

Chiefly this relates to the number of self-funded retirees the system is generating.

This final chapter sketches out some specific ideas to improve the system.

Each idea is ultimately designed to reduce the great super gap.

The Morrison Government already has an ambitious agenda to implement the significant reforms of the Hayne Commission. These ideas should be seen to be complementary.

POLICY IDEA 1
BREAK THE GREAT SUPER GAP WITH A TRUTH CAMPAIGN

The great super gap exists because of industry myths and misinformation. If we are to reach a 50 per cent self-funded target, the nation will need to hear the truth about their super.

Australians have been told that a 9 per cent super contribution is going to solve all their problems in retirement and that a 12 per cent payment would make it even better. This is not true for the bulk.

As the actuarial data demonstrates, there is no substitute for voluntary savings for Australians wishing to be self-funded.

Accordingly, as the beneficiaries of the mandatory superannuation scheme, the superannuation industry should be forced to invest in a truth campaign.

The truth campaign should include a clear visual representation of what a superannuation guarantee contribution will deliver in the form of a retirement provision.

The government could provide baseline assumptions to standardise communications and ensure projections were fair and reasonable.

This way Australians will have the information they need to determine whether to save more or less. It would blow away the myth that super will see people through their retirement.

Member statements and superannuation fund websites should contain the information. Fines paid by financial institutions could also contribute to the truth campaign.

POLICY IDEA 2
IMPROVE SYSTEM FLEXIBILITY

The 1992 workplace is long gone yet super is frozen in time. There should be more flexibility that takes labour force changes like the emergence of the gig economy into account.

Given the significant trade-off between increased super contributions and home ownership for lower income people, the First Home Super Saver Accounts Scheme should be broadened.

This is a relatively new structure which has performed well within its very limited constraints.

Australians should be allowed to use their mandatory superannuation contributions to purchase a first home, not solely the voluntary contributions. That way, people can decide what is best for them: a first home or a super account.

There is already a provision in place for early access to super on financial hardship grounds.

The COVID-19 crisis made it necessary for the Parliament to enact laws to enable Australians to access of up to $20,000 of their super. It allows for tranches of up to $10,000 over two consecutive financial years.

The impact of this change is relatively minimal and the funds have adequate liquidity to facilitate these withdrawals - as required under law.

Treasury estimates these measures will result in about $27 billion being withdrawn from a $3 trillion super system. That's less than 1 per cent of total super savings.

These new measures (or a derivation) need to be extended beyond COVID-19 to allow Australians easier access to their funds.

Maintaining a permanently widened early access scheme provides Australians facing financial difficulty with more resources to deal with challenges thrown up by life.

It will reduce the risk people will lose their home.

It is, after all the people's money as Treasurer Josh Frydenberg has repeatedly said during 2020.

POLICY IDEA 3
ESTABLISH A COMPETITIVE SYSTEM UNDERPINNED BY "SUPER GUARANTEE AUSTRALIA"

It is the clear the incumbent default funds have not used their privileged position to benefit workers. With returns lower than the Future Fund, the existing system cannot be maintained.

One option would be to open the system to more competition; effectively by letting more industry and retail funds compete for default status. However the ongoing indifference of employers and workers suggests this would have only limited impact in getting fees down and returns up.

As outlined, a simple default fund should be established: Super

Guarantee Australia. It could collect contributions and outsource investment management to established managers like the Future Fund.

This approach would significantly reduce cost and duplication and allow Australians access to a high quality scheme (through intermediation).

POLICY IDEA 4
AMEND THE SEX DISCRIMINATION ACT FOR WOMEN

The average superannuation balance in 2017-18 for men was $196,400 and $129,100 for women.

Men have nearly 40 per cent more super on average than women.

The Grattan Institute has identified two key reasons for this gender gap in retirement savings:

> First, women retire with comparatively less savings than men, resulting in relatively lower incomes in retirement. Second, women are at much greater risk of absolute poverty in retirement due to their smaller retirement savings, especially when they do not own their own home.

The super gender gap is persistent across all age groups to varying degrees of intensity and illustrates how the super system inadequately protects the interests of women.

Several reforms have been proposed to address the gender gap including increasing the Super Guarantee to 12 per cent or super top-ups.

Calls have been made to expedite the process of increasing the Superannuation Guarantee rate in the name of assisting female retirees but this is a blunt instrument like so many policies in the superannuation landscape.

The Superannuation Guarantee rate is scheduled to rise from 9.5 per cent to 12 per cent by July 2025.

However, 'higher compulsory super contributions are ultimately funded by lower wages, which means lower living standards for workers today.'

Considering that women on average earn less than men, increases in the Superannuation Guarantee will have a disproportionate effect on their spending capacity.

Calls have also been made to provide more top-ups to the super savings of low-income earners, with a particular emphasis on women.

Currently, the government provides two super top-ups for low-income workers – the Low Income Superannuation Tax Offset and The Super Co-contribution. Both of these top-ups provide low income earners with extra cash at a cost of $800 million and $160 million respectively.

Unlike pensions, eligibility for super top-ups depends only on the income of the individual super contributor. This means the top-ups also benefit low-income earners in high-income households

– think a cafe worker who may be married to an engineer.

Overall, proposals to boost the super savings of workers through increasing tax breaks or providing additional 'top-ups' will do nothing to help women in need.

As a contributory system, people get out what they put in. Men earn more than women and therefore put more into super than women. As such, men will retire with a bigger super nest than women.

Beating the women's super-gap requires targeted, not economy wide solutions.

That's why the Sex Discrimination Act should be amended to allow women to be paid a higher superannuation rate by employers which choose to contribute more.

Companies which are currently paying women more than men have been forced to obtain an exemption from the Act.

POLICY IDEA 5
JOINT SUPER ACCOUNTS

Large superannuation funds are not allowed to offer joint accounts. For economic reasons, the industry has argued to keep separate accounts, so higher and more fees can be charged.

We should move to establish accounts for families or couples. Two thirds of Australians are married when they are retired. Post-retirement, data shows that most marriages end with death rather than divorce.

There is already a model to follow in terms of how this could work: SMSFs are better designed to support combined super.

These accounts would provide accurate projections for couples and their retirement income, given that the pension is based on marital status. It would close the gender gap for women in retirement if they are financing together.

The current system of splitting contributions to a spouse is currently under-utilised and an "administrative burden." Making joint super accounts would mean super funds can remove this.

Couples can have the flexibility of a SMSF without the burden of managing it.

POLICY IDEA 6
FACILITATE VOLUNTARY CONTRIBUTIONS

Assuming the truth campaign works and more Australians are aware of how much they actually need to save, it would be desirable to look at the voluntary savings incentives. There are a range of schemes in place, from co-contributions to contribution caps, transition to retirement and salary sacrifice.

It is essential that these programmes are properly calibrated so that the scheme can deliver on its objective.

POLICY IDEA 7
ALLOWING LARGER SMSFs

Increasing the number of members from four to six in an SMSF would provide additional flexibility and choice in the superannuation system. It would also help reduce fees and costs.

Increasing the number would allow families with five and six members the ability to establish an SMSF together or allow the remaining members of a family to join an SMSF, which currently is an unavailable option to larger families.

Including more members in an SMSF is not likely to have a real effect on fees because SMSF fees are typically charged on a fixed administration basis regardless of the number of members and without consideration to the balance of the superannuation account.

Pooling super balances in one SMSF would avoid the costs of running separate SMSFs. Further, if the pool of assets is increased in an SMSF through including more members, then the SMSF would become more cost-efficient as the fees reduce as a percentage of the total assets of the fund. Another benefit from this spreading of fees across members is that lower income earning members could potentially have lower fees than they would in APRA-regulated superannuation funds.

With the reputations of many large retail and industry funds having been destroyed by the Hayne Royal Commission and COVID-19, the accessibility of SMSFs should be widened to more Australians.

POLICY IDEA 8
IMPROVE TRANSPARENCY

In a mandatory scheme, there should be a bias towards transparency. Yet we do not see the super funds disclosing the considerable payments which are made to related parties.

As this book has set out, the super funds are set to pay $31 million per annum to trade unions within a decade. Similarly, financial institutions with a superannuation licence should be required to disclose related party payments.

This incredible transfer of money should be disclosed so that members are armed with the information.

In annual reports and on websites, super funds should simply disclose payments to unions and related financial institutions. Similarly, if a super fund is fined by a regulator, the fund should be compelled to communicate the breach to members via email or a similar cost effective method.

CONCLUSION

The idea behind super remains sound. The execution has been poor.

It is a very large scheme. However it is not working hard enough for working Australians who fund the scheme.

The system is too introspective, expensive, driven by culture wars and defensive about change.

There is no point in having a vast scheme which does not allow or encourage the bulk of Australians to become self-funded retirees.

Yet so many of us believe that super will deliver a self-funded retirement when it won't.

The great super gap must be hit with the truth so that people can prepare accordingly with more or with fewer voluntary contributions.

The actuaries report the necessary contribution rate for an average worker is closer to 20 than 10 per cent. Thankfully, no Australian government would ever consider forcing workers to save 20 per cent into a fund without their consent.

The path to a better, sustainable super scheme is a combination of screwing down costs and fees, boosting competition and member transparency.

Unless Australians better understand the path we are on, how can we expect the system to work?

The truth campaign is essential and should be embraced by an industry which is privileged like no other in our country.

Otherwise, there should be more flexibility to recognise the economy has changed in the past few decades. There is more flexible work and home ownership is harder to achieve. Women still face an enormous superannuation gap.

The system should evolve to cater to diverse needs. Almost no other sector works with a static set of laws from three decades ago and the industry ought to look at reform as an opportunity to become sustainable.

The system itself needs a new market structure to drive fees down. The $32 billion bill Australians pay for super each year is more than Australians spend on power bills. This new system should have choice and simplicity at its heart with a government backstop.

The compulsion of the system compels policymakers to think harder about the outcomes than the political class has managed for the first 30 years of mandatory super.

Ultimately the nation has invested in super like nothing else. The cost of tax concessions demonstrate the taxpayer's commitment to the scheme. We must do all we can to get a better deal for workers from their super.

AFTERWORD

This short book has been a challenging project for a freshman Senator. I thought it was important to spend the precious time I have been granted in public office to advance an agenda which I had spoken about publicly for some time.

Certainly I did not want to wait for opportunities to come to me (they never do!), I wanted to create a policy discussion by generating a product.

After all, this is a role which is about policy.

This is a body of work which has the potential to drive the debate on super into sensible territory.

As I say in the outset, my test for whether this has been a productive use of time is if it drives the debate out of ideology and culture wars into solution mode. In other words, if we can have an honest debate about super and how it can be fixed, that would be a success in my opinion.

There are some good ideas in this monograph, many of which are not mine. The ideas have come from people who have helped me pull this together and I want to thank Michael Rice, Richard Gilbert and many others. All of these people read draft manuscripts, provided advice, guidance and helped me find errors.

My staff have been incredible in helping me pull together the paper. Brad McHugh, John Mangos, Marcus Harrington, Adam Yu helped with research, logistics and kept me sane.

Finally a big thanks to Will Nemesh, for providing the resources to fund the research for this project which was important for credibility.

NOTES

Introduction

1 Retirement Income Review Consultation Paper. The Treasury (Canberra: 2019). https://treasury.gov.au/sites/default/files/2019-11/c2019-36292-v2.pdf.

1 Big Money

1 Easson, Mary (2017). *Keating's & Kelty's super legacy : the birth and relentless threats to the Australian system of superannuation.* Connor Court Publishing, Redland Bay, Qld.

2 Bowen, Chris, (2013). *The Money Men: Australia's 12 Most Notable Treasurers.* Melbourne University Press, pp4-25.

3 Tilley, Paul: *A History of the Australian Treasury.* Melbourne University Publishing, Scoresby :, South Carlton, 2019.

4 Ibid.

5 "Public Pensions Are Woefully Underfunded." *The Economist,* 2019. https://www.economist.com/leaders/2019/11/16/public-pensions-are-woefully-underfunded?frsc=dg%7Ce.

6 Ibid.

7 Walsh, Peter (1995) *Confessions of a Failed Finance Minister.* Milsons Point, NSW: Random House.

8 Benson, Simon. "Unions Amass $1.5bn War Chest as Membership Falls." *The Australian,* September 6 2017. https://www.theaustralian.com.au/nation/unions-amass-15bn-war-chest-as-their-membership-falls-away/news-story/387917d6e0cdcfb227b3e59ffe62488f.

9 Australian Electoral Commission, 2020. Trade Unions as Associated Entities (online) available at https://www.aec.gov.au, accessed May 7, 2020.

10 David Marin-Guzman, "Fo.rmer NUW boss Derrick Belan guilty of $650,000 union fraud", March 23, 2018, *The Australian Financial Review,* https://www.afr.com/policy/economy/former-nuw-boss-derrick-belan-guilty-of-650000-union-fraud-20180323-h0xw8r.

11 ASIC (2008), Financial Advice: Vertically Integrated Institutions and Conflicts of Interest, Report 562. Canberra, pp.6-7.

12 Financial Advice: Vertically Integrated Institutions and Conflicts of Interest. ASIC (Canberra: 2018). https://download.asic.gov.au/media/4632718/rep-562-published-24-january-2018.pdf.

13 Hayne Royal Commission testimony (Regan).

14　McIlroy, Tom. "Frydenberg Moves on Royal Commission Mortgage Broker Recommendations." *Australian Financial Review,* August 26 2019. https://www.afr.com/politics/federal/frydenberg-moves-on-royal-commission-mortgage-broker-recommendations-20190825-p52kke.

2 Conflicts

1　Neil, M (2020) Hostplus CEO Defends Tennis Entertainment. (Online) *The Courier.* https://thecourier.com.au, accessed May 8, 2020.

2　*Australian Financial Review,* (2020) Industry Super ambush Government with 3.5 million campaign (online) www.afr.com, accessed May 8, 2020.

3　Benson, Simon. "Industry Super Fund Reverses Stance on Franking Credits." *The Australian,* February 11 2019. https://www.theaustralian.com.au/nation/industry-super-fund-reverses-stance-on-franking-credits/news-story/fa1f-66176d279af1cd707048df7f16b8.

4　"SMSF Statistics: 1.1 Million Members with $747bn in Super." SuperGuide, Updated June 14, 2019, https://www.superguide.com.au/smsfs/smsfs-lead-the-super-pack-again.3https://www.industrysuper.com/media/dividend-imputation-chang- es-sensible-but-savings-should-be-reinvested-to-modernise-super/

5　https://www.aph.gov.au/Parliamentary_Business/Committees/House/ Economics/FrankingCredits/Submissions - Wilson Asset Management Submission

6　Industry SuperFunds. "Dividend Imputation Changes Sensible but Savings Should Be Reinvested to Modernise Super." news release, March 13, 2018, https://www.industrysuper.com/media/dividend-imputation-changes-sensible-but-savings-should-be-reinvested-to-modernise-super/.

7　"Aged pension more effective in retirement than 'failed' super", *The Australian,* February 2, 2020, https://www.theaustralian.com.au/business/aged-pension-more-effective-in-retirement-than-failed-super/news-story/ffadc88b-4c4e678399a9cb7de09af683

8　Colebatch, Hal (2012). *The modest member : the life and times of Bert Kelly.* Connor Court Publishing, Ballan, Vic

3 Objectives

1　"Retirement Income Review Consultation Paper." The Treasury, 2019.

2　ABS, Household Income and Wealth, 2017-2018, Table 13.3.

3　https://treasury.gov.au/sites/default/files/2019-03/2015_IGR.pdf-note 2013-14 = 70%, 2055 = 67%

4　Speech by the Hon. P. J. Keating, MP, ALP Campaign Launch, 14 February, 1996, https://pmtranscripts.pmc.gov.au/sites/default/files/original/00009942.pdf

5　World Bank national accounts data, and OECD National Accounts data files. Gross domestic savings (% of GDP), https://data.worldbankorg/indicator/N Y.GDS.TOTL.ZS?end=2018&locations=AU&start=1974

6　"Superannuation and the economy", June 2015, The Association of Superannuation Funds of Australia (ASFA), https://www.superannuation.asn.au/Articledocuments/359/1506-Super_tax_concessions_and_economy.pdf.aspx?Embed=Y

7   International Monetary Fund, International Financial Statistics and Balance of Payments databases, World Bank, International Debt Statistics, and World Bank and OECD GDP estimates, Foreign direct investment, net inflows (% of GDP), https://data.worldbank.org/indicator/BX.KLT.DINV.WD.GD.ZS

8   Chris Pash, "Australians are now paying a massive $32 billion a year in super fund fees", *Business Insider Australia*, October 18, 2018. https://www.businessinsider.com.au/superannuation-super-fees-rise-32-billion-a-year-2018-10

9   'Superannuation: Assessing Efficiency and Competitiveness. Productivity Commission Inquiry Report' (page 14 overview). Productivity Commission. Australian Government. December 21, 2018: https://www.pc.gov.au/inquiries/completed/superannuation/assessment/report/superannuation-assessment.pdf

10   Ros Stephens, "Super tax concessions: what's behind the curtain?" KPMG Insights, 19 April 2018, https://home.kpmg/au/en/home/insights/2018/04/superannuation-tax-concessions-19-april-2018.html

11   Paul Keating, A Retirement Incomes Policy, address to the Australian Graduate School of Management, 25 July, 1992, https://parlinfo.aph.gov.au/parlInfo/search/display/display.w3p;query=Id%3A%22media%2Fpressrel%2FU69F6%22.

12   https://grattan.edu.au/wp-content/uploads/2018/11/912-Money-in-retirement.pdf p. 37

13   Tilley, op.cit., p. 252.

14   https://www.ricewarner.com/wp-content/uploads/2019/06/Rpt-What-is-the-right-level-of-SG-Actuaries-Institute-June-2019.pdf pg 20

15   https://www.apra.gov.au/quarterly-superannuation-statistics

4 The Big Super Trade off

1   Housing in an ageing Australia: Nest and nest egg? htt CEPAR research brief, November 2019, ps:// www. firstlinks. com. au/ uploads/ 201911 / cepar- re search-brief-housing-ageing-australia.pdf.

2   Daley et al (2019) Money in Retirement: More than Enough, Grattan Institute, p.64.

3   ABS, Housing Occupancy and Costs, 1981-2011: First Home Buyers in Australia (cat. no.4103.0.55.001).

4   Daley et al, op.cit. p.27.

5   The Treasury, Retirement Income Review, 22 November 2019 - 03 February 2020Consultation Paper https://www.treasury.gov.au/consultation/c2019-36292

6   Daley et al, op.cit., p.40.

5 Who Actually Pays

1   Productivity Commission Inquiry Report, Superannuation: Assessing Efficiency and Competitiveness, No. 91, 21 December 2018, https://www.pc.gov.au/in-

quiries/completed/superannuation/assessment/report/superannuation-assessment.pdf
2   Ibid.

6 The System

1   McDonald et al, Digital Platform Work in Australia: Preliminary Findings from a National Survey, Victorian Department of Premier and Cabinet, (2019) p.30.

7 No Choice, No Competition

1   Australian Electoral Commission, 2020. Trade Unions as Associated Entities, (Online), available at: https://www.aec.gov.au, accessed May 7, 2020.
2   Cooper et al (2010), Super System Review: Final Report, Part 1 - Overview and Recommendations, Department of Treasury, Canberra, P. 9.
3   David Crowe, "MTAA sparks industry super inquiry", *Australian Financial Review*, June 10, 2011 https://www.afr.com/policy/economy/mtaa-sparks-industry-super-in- quiry-20110610-icqza
4   OECD (2010) Review of Regulatory Reform in Australia, p 66.
5   Hall, A (2015) The Australian's Current Government Debt Position. Flagpost, Australian Parliamentary Library, pp.2-4.
6   futurefund.gov.au, (2020) Future Fund Investment Performance (online - accessed May 7, 2020.
7   APRA, (2020) Myu Super Product Heat Map, (online at www.apra.gov.au, accessed, May 7, 2020).
8   Martin, T. W. (2016) What Does Nevada's $35 Billion Fund Manager Do All Day? Nothing. *Wall Street Journal Online*, October 19 2019, www.wsj.com.

8 The Kit and Caboodle

1   Productivity Commission (2018) Superannuation: Assessing Efficiency and Competitiveness, Report No. 91. Canberra, pp. 161-163.
2. Ibid., pp 16-17.